EXCOMMUNICATED

11 Steps to Church Revitalization

Danny Burnley

ISBN: 978-1-940645-35-3

100 Manly Street
Greenville, South Carolina

PRINTED IN THE UNITED STATES OF AMERICA

Praise for *Excommunicated: 11 Steps to Church Revitalization*

The Lord asked Ezekiel, "Can the bones live?' Ezekiel answered, "O Lord God, Thou knowest." The answer is yes. God can revive His people and His church. There are definitely steps that must be taken for a turnaround to occur in a declining church. Danny Burnley has been used by God to implement these steps in several churches, and God has been seen bringing new life to His churches. We must return to the main things of soul-winning and discipleship.

— PAUL FLEMING, executive pastor, Forestville Baptist Church, Greenville, South Carolina

---

It is my privilege to commend Dr. Danny Burnley and his ministry of Church Revitalization Consulting. I have known Brother Danny since 1994. He possesses the character of Barnabas, "the encourager." I have watched him pray for, encourage and partner with discouraged pastors and declining, dying churches with great success. In the area of church revitalization, Danny is not a theoretician, but a genuine, proven practitioner. I've observed as he's stepped down from very healthy, successful churches to embrace struggling churches. Under his leadership, those churches have experienced true turnaround by becoming healthy and following God's prescribed pattern for growth. I'm confident Dr. Danny Burnley's wisdom and proven leadership can be a blessing to your church in this day of decline.

— MIKE MOODY, senior pastor, Honea Path First Baptist Church, Honea Path, South Carolina

---

Danny Burnley has the skills, experience and the anointing of the Holy Spirit to lead much larger churches, but his heart and his calling are for helping small, struggling churches to emerge from the spiritual doldrums to fulfill the Great Commission and make disciples of Jesus. I have watched him for several years lead hurting churches through the healing process and emerge on the other side with a stronger unity and a stronger focus on reaching people for Christ. And I am thankful that he still yearns to help even more churches by publishing this book. Read this book, and you will not only learn effective strategies, but you will also hear his heart. Thank you, Danny!

— WADE LEONARD, senior pastor, Mauldin First Baptist Church, Mauldin, South Carolina

---

To a humble heart, the devoted Dr. Danny Burnley, "But do not forget to do good and to share, for with such sacrifices God is well pleased" (Hebrews 13:16). To know Pastor Burnley is such a privilege. His directions for a holy and obedient life are well worth hearing. This book, *Excommunicated: 11 Steps to Church Revitalization*, is more than a blessing and is the answer to many prayers. Because of Pastor Burnley's caring heart and his desire to help others, I am reminded of the scripture for which he is well-deserving: "Give, and it will be given to you; a good measure, pressed down, shaken together and running over, will be poured into your lap. For with the measure you use, it will be measured to you." We are more than grateful for all you have done to help us here at Hosannah Baptist Church. Your kindness and generosity have sustained us and will forever be in our hearts.

— CLYDE D. CANNON, pastor, Hosannah Baptist Church, McCormick, South Carolina

---

Danny Burnley has a great gift and special anointing of God to serve the body of Christ. He has a ministry to struggling churches and helps them to rebound and become strong again. He helps bring life to something that is dying. Danny has been a great help to me and to my church leaders by giving strategic suggestions that were easy to follow and accomplish. God was able to do a miracle in our lives and the life of our church. Through this process, I personally have gained a great friend and encourager.

— GREG FORTUNE, pastor, East Park Baptist Church, Greenville, South Carolina

"And ye shall know the truth, and the truth shall make you free" (John 8:32). Within these pages, you will find many years of dedicated preaching and the study of God's Word. Brother Danny has put to pen those truths that God has revealed to him while working with God's Church all of these years. I have witnessed Danny put this knowledge of God's plan for His church to work many times. I thank my God that I might gain years of knowledge from the reading of this book.

— WESLEY A. POOLE, deacon, Siloam Baptist Church, Easley, South Carolina

---

I have known Dr. Danny Burnley for about thirty years. In that time, he has been my mentor, both as a pastor and as a friend. He has a deep desire to see the lost saved — in fact, he witnessed to me. But that is matched only by his love of the church and his desire to see true spiritual growth. I have seen him stay the course with a godly zeal, whether it was a Romanian mission trip, preaching a church growth revival or ministering to a young pastor who was greatly in need of an encouraging word.

— PHIL KEOWN, pastor, Lake Russell Baptist Church, Elberton, Georgia

---

When Dr. Danny Burnley came to Laurel Baptist Church, our church had declined continuously in membership and attendance. As I watched our church (God's Church) decline, I realized I could not be on the sidelines anymore. I began to pray that God would use me in any way that I could serve and help this cause. By the time Dr. Burnley arrived, LBC had changed from a committee-led church to a ministry-led church, at his suggestion. This was all new to me, and I really did not want to be in a ministry, so I began to drag my feet. I even told Pastor Burnley that I was not going to sign up for any ministries, but then I remembered that I had been praying for God to use me. How could I pray to be used by God and then refuse to get involved? Pastor Burnley asked me to become one of his prayer partners, and through God getting my attention, and receiving direction and encouragement from Pastor Burnley, joy began to fill my soul and my attitude began to change. Now God has opened a door for me to teach God's Word in a

Bible Study Group, and I love it! If you will turn to God's Word and will also apply the principles of this book, you and your church will be revitalized!

— JOHN MULLIS, deacon, Laurel Baptist Church, Greenville, South Carolina

---

If your church is not growing, it would be a great benefit to read this book and see how Dr. Burnley used these methods to completely revive Laurel Baptist Church. We were only months away from closing the doors, with less than forty active members. Now our church is growing, with over 200 active members, and there is an excitement about our future.

— SANDRA CLARK, prayer partner, Laurel Baptist Church, Greenville, South Carolina

DEDICATION

This book is dedicated to my precious wife, Laverne, who has faithfully served by my side for over forty-seven years. She is a wonderful wife, mother, grandmother and pastor's companion.

I also thank God for my mentors over the years: Rev. Dallas Suttles and Rev. Charles Lavender, who were my advisors and pastors; evangelist Aubert Rose, who taught me, prayed for me and helped order my ministry through his wise counsel; Delano McMinn, who believed that God had gifted me with the ministry of working with troubled churches, and who called on me, challenged me and supported me fully; evangelist Rick Ingle, who preached revivals and taught me how to plan, prepare and promote revivals; Harold Hunter, who served as pastor, evangelist and president of Trinity College of the Bible and Trinity Theological Seminary, and who always encouraged and challenged me and edified the Lord Jesus Christ through his preaching. He too has been such a friend. I am also grateful for the ministry of Sam Cathey and the powerful sermon he preached, "Five Things You Must Do to Have the Fire of God to Fall." This sermon revolutionized my life and ministry. I am also grateful to Bishop Leon Stewart, a blind Pentecostal preacher who preached one day at Emmanuel College in Franklin Springs, Georgia, on the subject, "How to Take Your Mountain." This was at my lowest time in ministry. From that sermon, God began an experience I shall never forget.

To all who taught me in Sunday school, and to my every pastor, deacon, prayer partner and support, "I thank my God upon every remembrance of you" (Philippians 1:3).

A special thanks to Rita McIntyre, office manager at Laurel Baptist Church, for all her typing and organizing of this book, and to June Roper, who proofread and finalized the preparation of this book for printing.

FOREWORD

I write as a personal acquaintance of Dr. Danny Burnley for the past thirty-two years and as one who has observed his fruitful ministry of leading very troubled churches, many of which looked hopeless, to a renewed life and fruitfulness. It is very obvious that God not only called him to preach and pastor, but also gifted him with special abilities to lead dying churches to new life in obeying Christ's Great Commission. As a minister of the gospel for sixty-five years and involved in church growth, it has been amazing to see firsthand how God has used Danny in all the churches he has pastored to completely revitalize them.

I met Danny and his fine family in 1983 in Iva, South Carolina, at his invitation to assist him in a church growth revival. I observed his ability to rally people to cooperate in doing big things for God and was blessed to return to every church he has served since to assist him in church growth (often more than once at each place). I saw God use him equally at different churches. I did a ten-year historical analysis of each church and found steep decline in all areas, which indicated they were in bad shape and headed for death unless something happened. And something did happen! God sent Danny Burnley, whom He has specially equipped to turn churches around to obedience and application of the Great Commission.

It is sad to have to say that many churches in America today are in decline, including many of our Southern Baptist Convention churches. If something isn't done to correct this, many of them will not continue to survive, much less grow. All churches are either growing or declining, none remain the same for long. It is God's will for all of His churches to be healthy and growing, and they can be. This hinges on leadership. Danny Burnley, endowed and proven by God, knows what it takes to lead a sick and dying church back to vitality, both spiritually and numerically. He has shared these principles in two books and is also making himself available as God enables him to assist churches in their desire for revitalization. This second book is a sequel to *Spiritual Strokes*, which I also highly recommend.

I am quite sure that you and your church will never be the same, but will be much better, when you let Dr. Danny Burnley assist you, through his books or in person, to continue our Lord's Great Commission through His local churches.

Aubert Rose
Church Growth Evangelist (retired)
Benton, Kentucky

TABLE OF CONTENTS

Chapter 1	Excommunicated	13
Chapter 2	Rebuilding the Wall	23
Chapter 3	Setting Up a Dream Team	31
Chapter 4	Developing a 20/20 Vision	41
Chapter 5	Establishing a Church Growth Calendar	49
Chapter 6	Dissolving Spiritual Blood Clots (Part 1)	61
Chapter 7	Dissolving Spiritual Blood Clots (Part 2)	71
Chapter 8	Dealing with Spiritual Strokes	83
Chapter 9	Creating Balance Within the Church	97
Chapter 10	Building Up Bible Fellowship	109
Chapter 11	Transitioning to Ministries	121
Chapter 12	Promoting Missions More Effectively	135
Chapter 13	Planning a Church Revitalization Crusade	147

Chapter One

EXCOMMUNICATED

Behold, how good and how pleasant it is for brethren to dwell together in unity! (Psalm 133:1)

It was in 1975 on a Wednesday evening at my home church. We usually had a midweek prayer service, but on this night a special business meeting had been scheduled. I remember the parking lot and the auditorium being nearly filled to capacity. Instead of praying, my wife and I, in our mid-twenties at that time, were excommunicated, along with several others.

Now, I realize that "excommunicated" is not a term we normally associate with a Baptist church, but that is exactly what happened that night — we were formally disassociated from our church. We were, for all practical purposes, excommunicated.

This was one of the saddest nights of my life — not because of the excommunication, but for the hurt and damage it caused to the church, to the families and to the community. Here was a wonderful church that had suffered a terrible spiritual stroke. As the result of this one meeting, families were divided, parents and children were divided, a large number of the members left the church, and there were some who never attended a church after that night. Even to this day, there are many scars that still remain.

Looking back on that night, I have come to realize that this was both the worst and best thing that ever happened to me as a born-again believer in Jesus Christ. It was the worst thing because it was much like a divorce. Over the years, we have all witnessed young couples who had fallen in love. They started out well in their marriage until one day, because of adultery, or lack of time together, debt, misplaced priorities or for other reasons, their marriage ended in a bitter divorce. Both husband and wife had to go through heartache, pain, sadness and sorrow. The children suffered emotionally, and there was an aftereffect on everyone. A divorce or a church split are the nearest experiences to the death of a loved one. These truly hurt everyone, including the church and the testimony for Christ throughout the community. There is no winner in a church division.

You may have noticed by now that the name of this church has not been mentioned. The reason for this is that I do not want to hurt these dear people, as they have already been hurt over these years. I loved them then, I love them now, and I always will love them in Jesus Christ.

Yes, this was one of the worst experiences of my life, but it has also turned out to be one of the best experiences. You may be asking how this can be. The answer is that through all of this, God has taught me valuable lessons, and His precious Word has come alive!

Let us remember, in Genesis 45, Joseph, who was sold into slavery by his own brothers. After Joseph had been in slavery and through numerous fiery trials, he was eventually promoted, second only to Pharoah. When he revealed himself to his brothers in verses 7 and 8, he said, "And God sent me before you to preserve you a posterity in the earth, and to save your lives by a great deliverance. So now it was not you that sent me hither, but God; and he hath made me a father to Pharoah, and lord of all his house, and a ruler throughout all the land of Egypt." Joseph was saying to his brothers that what had happened was meant for his harm, yet God had used the episode for His glory and to be a blessing to His own people.

Here it is today, some forty years after my excommunication, and God has given to me a heart and ministry to help hurting and struggling churches. Today God has allowed me to write this book to encourage the saints, pastors, teachers and churches. These lessons were never learned in a seminary, but by the working of God's Holy Spirit through trials and disappointments.

Remember, my friend, some 80 percent of our churches are either stagnant or in a decline. It is my desire to share with all churches how God can revitalize your spirit and your church. God can put you back on the right path, and you can experience again the joy and excitement as the body of Christ.

Take a moment to understand what happened in my home church. How could such a church end up in such a mess? We need to know the answer in order to understand the following eleven chapters.

First, let us consider the beginning of my home church. Back in the 1950s, the First Baptist Church in my hometown asked for volunteers from their membership to go into a new subdivision and begin a new mission work. My parents, along with others, were willing to go. About the time of the beginning of this new work, I was conceived in my mother's womb. From that time until now, I have always been in or near the church. Our family was always in church on Sunday mornings for both Sunday school and worship and returning Sunday evenings for discipleship training and worship, Wednesday prayer services, and for all revival services unless we were sick. My mother was the pianist until my dad had his stroke years later. My brother then became our pianist. Our family was always involved in the church.

There was never a time when we had a preacher or teacher to question God's Holy Word. All the preachers and leaders stood on the Bible as God's authority. We believed that Jesus Christ was the Son of God, that He died on the cross for our sins, and that He was buried and arose again the third day according to the scriptures. Our church believed in the major doctrines of the Bible, preached God's holy Word, believed the Bible from cover to cover — and believed the cover: The Bible! This congregation promoted evangelism and promoted worldwide missions and was doctrinally sound. If there was ever a church that loved God, loved the church and loved lost souls, it was our home church. It was the desire of this church to bring honor and glory to our Lord and Savior, Jesus Christ.

The reason for my pointing out all of this to you is because, like so many of our churches today, something went terribly wrong. What could it have been? What caused this division?

Secondly, let us now consider what went wrong. Having been a pastor now for some thirty-seven years and having witnessed a number of churches in this same situation, I have discovered several common denominators. All churches that begin anew under God's leadership will begin to grow spiritually and numerically. They start with a humble beginning, praying, trusting God, studying and teaching the scriptures and seeking for lost souls. Usually they begin without a worship center, very little or no financial support, little or no staff — just a simple step of faith in God and His Word. They begin humbly on their knees and emphasize prayer, calling upon God and depending on His Holy Word.

The church begins to grow, and souls are saved and baptized. The church is thrilled. Worship and praise sounds forth! The church becomes so busy with new ideas — man's ideas. Buildings are needed, bylaws are drawn up and added to, open business meetings are organized, and budgets are formed. We seem to have it altogether now — buildings, bylaws, business meetings and budgets. With everyone becoming so involved with meetings and more meetings, we become so busy that there is very little time anymore for prayer and emphasis on the Word of God. When the prayers of the Saints cease, the flesh takes over. Carnality begins to set in, man's ideas and priorities take over, and soon leaders are chosen who have little or no spirituality. Some of these leaders could care little or not at all about prayer meetings, Sunday school, Bible study or being involved in reaching lost souls. Because of the lack of knowledge of God's Word, spiritual blood clots begin to develop.

It is so interesting to note at the time of our church division, we were growing numerically, and those days were the most exciting for me. During this period of time, God began dealing with me and with my heart. I had learned so much through the pastor who was serving with us. He had the gift of administration. Through the preaching of God's Holy Word, I began examining myself as a church member.

When I was a young boy, around ten years of age, my best friend, Brooks Bennette, and I would always sit together during worship services. One Sunday morning at the invitation, Brooks turned to me and said, "Move. I want to be saved." He stepped out into the aisle and began approaching the pastor. I decided I, too, would join the church. That is exactly what happened. Brooks was saved, and I joined the church. We were both baptized together, and there we were both church members.

As I began to grow up as a teenager, my dad had his stroke, and I became bitter. Thank God, I do not have to tell you how sinful I became. At church, I looked like a little angel to so many, but the truth was I was a spiritual blood clot within the church. I was trying to hold on to God with one hand and the devil with the other hand.

One particular lady asked me one Sunday if I had ever done anything wrong. She shared with me that her Sunday school class discussed my lifestyle, and they thought I was such a wonderful young person and role model. Unknown to them, my life was a poor example for anyone. My life had grown worse and worse, until one Sunday evening when a guest preacher filled in during the absence of our pastor, and he simply preached the same gospel I had heard numerous times before. It was on this night that the Holy Spirit truly convicted me of my sins and caused me to realize that Jesus was not Lord of my life. When the invitation was given, I bowed my head and with my heart prayed, "Oh God, I know I am a sinner, and I do not want to play church anymore. I am sorry for all my sins, and I ask for you to forgive me. Come into my heart, Lord Jesus. I want you to be my Savior and Lord."

I immediately stepped into the aisle and went straight to the preacher to tell him that I was a church member and had been baptized, but I had never truly repented of my sins until then. I explained my prayer to Jesus Christ and my faith in Him as my Savior and Lord. I wanted to be baptized biblically. He shared this with the church, and my life began a transformation with a desire to serve Him. I was no longer just a church member, but I was saved and part of the family of God!

After growing in the Lord for some time, the nominating committee asked me to teach a Sunday school class for twelve-to-thirteen-year-olds. Later, they wanted me to become the Royal Ambassador director. God blessed these ministries, with souls being saved and children, youth and their parents uniting with our church. I went on to become the youth Sunday school director and, finally, a deacon. I was on a spiritual high and could not get enough of God's word. It was a joy to share and to teach the Bible.

Now, here is where my heart began to break. After being ordained as a deacon, it wasn't long before I realized there was friction between the deacons and the pastor. All of these men, including my pastor, had been great mentors to me. These were my real heroes of the faith. I loved them all, and I still do.

I just could not understand why they could not get along with one another. For months, the friction began to grow, and the dissension began to spill over into the church. The Holy Spirit was being quenched. These were men of God, men who all these years prayed together, served together, visited the lost together and loved one another. This was so heart-wrenching. Why could we not all forgive and forget?

Any believer in Christ who goes through this experience will tell you that everyone involved will be affected. It will affect your sleep, your joy, your thoughts, your peace, your family and your entire church. Having such a burden for my church, I prayed and prayed. One day, while reading my Bible, I came across Matthew 5:23-24: "Therefore if thou bring thy gift to the altar, and there rememberest that thy brother have aught against thee; leave there thy gift before the altar, and go thy way; first be reconciled to thy brother, and then come and offer thy gift." I thought, "Praise God! There is the answer." It was so clear. I soon called my pastor and set up an appointment with him after the following evening service. I was so excited about our meeting and about the scripture.

When we met together in his study, I anxiously shared the scripture from Matthew 5 and asked him if we could somehow plan a reconciliation service, with everyone coming together, praying together and forgiving one another. I shared with him my love for my pastor, our deacons and for the entire church. After opening my heart to him, he responded by saying, "I am not in the begging business. If someone wants me to forgive them, let them come and ask me, and I will forgive them." As I returned home, it became a long, disappointing and sleepless night. My heart was so saddened.

During the next Sunday morning service, my heart was so heavy. Oh, if only we could all be reconciled and begin afresh! I thought about our Lord Jesus Christ as He hung there on the cruel cross with His outstretched arms, crying out to His Father, "Father, forgive them for they know not what they do" (Luke 23:23). As my pastor approached the pulpit and began to prepare to preach, he shared with the congregation that one of our deacons met with him last Sunday night after services and told him how to pastor this church. Everyone present knew that this person was me. They did not realize, however, that all I wanted to do was have a time of forgiveness and reconciliation.

From that day on, I was rejected by so many. Weeks passed, and I realized I was not wanted there. I surely did not want to raise my hand against God's anointed, so there was no other way to go but to begin seeking another church in which to serve. I was contacted soon afterward by another member, informing me that I would be excommunicated from my home church. Yes, this did happen, and God has taught me so many lessons since. Today, I still hold on to Matthew 5:23-24, and I still continue to pray for my home church. Over the years, I have mailed Christmas cards, letting them know the love I have for them. At times when traveling back home, I find myself in their church parking lot praying for them.

After our excommunication, my church held a revival service. My young little boy and I attended one of the services. The guest preacher preached on the love of Christ. My son and I sat on the back pew. In the middle of the sermon, the preacher stopped, looked back to where I was sitting and said to the congregation, "Do you all see that young man on the back row with the brown coat holding the little boy? Young man, I love you. I'm glad you are here tonight, and I know you love us because you are here." Everyone present knew who I was except the visiting revival preacher.

As time passed, a new church start began organizing, and I became a member. By God's grace, He allowed me to serve as their first deacon chairman. I began a new Sunday school class for young adults. Now, to all readers, please do not miss this! I worked hard to build a Sunday school class spiritually, numerically and prayerfully. After all this time, there were only three or four people present each Lord's Day for my class. What was wrong? I was doing everything possible, but my class would not grow. As I searched my own heart and life, God began to reveal my need to practice Matthew 5:23-24. As deacon chairman and a Sunday school teacher, the power of God seemed so far away.

Our pastor in this new church would preach and give an invitation. When we would sing the old song, "I Surrender All," or "Ready," I would stop singing, because I knew God was convicting me to surrender to His call to pastor and to preach. Think of the words from the song "Ready": "Ready to go, ready to stay, ready my place to fill. Ready for service, lowly or great, ready to do His will." To be ready meant surrendering my all to Jesus!

It was late one night when I went to this church all alone — just Jesus and me. I fell on my knees at the altar and began to plead with God for His power. I prayed for my former home church, confessing my sins and hard feelings toward those members. God said for me to pray for them and to bless them, but I did not know how, so I asked God to bless them and to take away my anger. I said, "Lord, here I am. Use me for your glory."

At a Wednesday prayer service, a young couple, Dwayne and Liz Humphrey, visited our church. We invited them to our new young adult class. They came the following Sunday, united with our class and joined our church. Today that same couple is there. Dwayne became our organist, and Liz holds several positions in the church by being a soul-winner for Christ! Our Sunday school class grew from three to thirty-three in only a few months.

As I began to experience God in my life, God revealed to me that these things that happened to me were for the advancement of His kingdom. Upon entering the ministry to prepare and to preach the gospel, my burden has always been to help those churches that are struggling with the same issues that faced my home church. It has also been my desire to help churches change and adjust from the status quo to become an exciting church for God's glory. A church does not have to be a megachurch, but just a church that honors our Lord.

You should know that after some twenty-five years in the ministry and as a pastor, I received a call to go back to my home church and preach a homecoming service! Twelve more years later I was invited back to preach another homecoming. I believe that a reconciliation service may be just around the corner! Pray for my home church, for God to work in and through it in a mighty way.

Lastly, where do you go from here? I call upon you to read the following eleven chapters and apply the eleven steps for church revitalization. It is an amazing and exciting journey! Think about it, my friend. If it had not been for my being excommunicated, this book might never have been written, and I would never have been able to challenge you and your church. Your best days can be ahead.

Be blessed in the name of Jesus! God wants to revitalize you and your church!

"Having therefore these promises, dearly beloved, let us cleanse ourselves from all filthiness of the flesh and spirit, perfecting holiness in the fear of God" (2 Corinthians 7:1).

Chapter Review: Excommunicated

Psalm 133:1

Consider the beginning of a church

What goes wrong within the church?

Where do we go from here?
    Matthew 5:23-24
    2 Corinthians 7:1

Chapter Two

REBUILDING THE WALL

And it came to pass when I heard these words, that I sat down and wept, and mourned certain days and fasted and prayed before the God of heaven. (Nehemiah 1:4)

If any believer or any church desires to see a spiritual renewal or revitalization of your church, then study the books of Nehemiah and Titus!

By reading Nehemiah, you will discover that he was not a pastor or an evangelist. He was simply an ordinary man of God, someone we would call, in our day, a layman. He served as the king's cupbearer. Before the time of his service, God's chosen people had been called to be a witness against idolatry; instead, they themselves had fallen and had become idolaters. As a result, God allowed them to be overtaken by the Babylonians.

As you read the book of Nehemiah, you will find that it was this layman who rebuilt the walls of Jerusalem and cleansed the temple. During the years of my ministry, I have come to realize that God can, and will, raise up a layman to do a great work rebuilding the wall of a church.

For this to become a reality, it must begin with a spirit of realization (1:3). Observe Nehemiah closely. In chapter 1, we find him faithful at his royal post when he received distressing news that "the wall of Jerusalem is broken down, and its gates are destroyed by fire." Notice first and foremost his reaction to this catastrophe. Nehemiah was told that a remnant — that is, a small number — were still there in the province and that they were in "great affliction and reproach." The "wall of Jerusalem was broken down and the gates were burned with fire" (Nehemiah 1:3).

The spirit of realization caused Nehemiah to react with a spirit of consecration (1:4). When Nehemiah heard these words, he sat down and wept, and mourned certain days and fasted, and prayed before the God of heaven.

The very reason I write this book is simply because this is how I feel about many of our churches today. My heart breaks over what we know to be a reality. A few churches across our land are known as megachurches. Praise God for these, but let us remember that some 80 percent of our churches are either in a decline or in a stagnant condition. Many within our congregations have chosen to leave their home churches and unite with a megachurch. At the same time, we have seen fewer men of God surrendering to preach the gospel or to be a pastor. Fewer numbers are willing to care for our nurseries, our children, and our youth. Many have left their churches in order to attend one service each week, where they have little or no responsibility. Baptisms are down in spite of our booming population. We have fewer missionaries, and funds to send missionaries are decreasing.

We have deacons, teachers and even staff members who do not have a clue as to how to lead a lost sinner to Christ. Very few leaders know the books of the Bible, and many today are blind to the doctrines of the Bible; therefore, the morals across our land are becoming like those of Sodom and Gomorrah!

Hosea 4:6 states: "My people are destroyed for lack of knowledge; because thou hast rejected knowledge, I will reject thee, that thou shalt be no priest to me; seeing thou hast forgotten the law of the God, I will also forget thy children." It seems as if the thinking of many churches today is, "Come as you are and leave as you were." As we look at the spiritual condition of America, we, too, should fall on our knees, weep and mourn over our precious land. We should fast and pray as did Nehemiah and seek the God of heaven. Our hearts should be broken over the spiritual and moral condition of our churches. Remember, God did not say that lost politicians, entertainers, Hollywood, or lost people should humble themselves. Yes, they should, but it begins with us, the church of our Lord Jesus. God tells us: "If my people which are called by my name shall humble themselves and pray, and seek my face, and turn from their wicked ways, then will I hear from heaven, I will forgive their sin and will heal their land" (2 Chronicles 7:14).

Like Nehemiah, we can be used of God to revitalize our churches when we have that experience of realization that moves us to the spirit of consecration. The answer to church revitalization is as simple as the plan of salvation!

If we want to see a revitalization of our churches, we must follow Nehemiah's example. He was a man of prayer. It was his nature to turn to God in moments of distress or victory. He immediately prayed when he heard Hanani's report. His heart went out to God for his dear people.

Today, after nearly forty years of service as a pastor, I have prayed and asked God what I can do to help the local church. I praise Him for the opportunities He has given me to serve in the local church. It has been my desire all these years to help churches that are struggling. It is such a joy to work with a local church that feels defeated and hopeless and to witness their renewal of hope, joy and excitement as they begin seeing God move in their midst. Oh what a joy it is!

Over the past two or three years, however, it has concerned me how little has been accomplished through my ministry in this area. He has, no doubt, laid upon my heart a desire to write this book, and I believe God will use it to help not just a few, but many, churches as they experience revitalization. These twelve simple chapters can cause any church to refocus, to dream again, and to witness God's working anew in their midst. Your church may never become a megachurch, but it can become a God-pleasing church when the Holy Spirit manifests Himself again!

Now, with your spirit of realization and consecration, allow me to offer you a biblical proposition that will definitely put you and your church on the right path. Take note that Nehemiah took the initiative. He said, in Nehemiah 1:5: "I beseech thee, O Lord of heaven, the great and terrible God."

First of all, will you — that's right, will you, the reader — be willing to fall on your knees before God and cry out to Him on your own behalf and on behalf of your church? Will you be a Nehemiah and seek to do God's will? Take note, my friend: Nehemiah not only prayed, he also made confession. He included himself by saying: "We have dealt very corruptly against Thee, and have not kept the commandments, nor the statutes, nor the judgments." Nehemiah included himself in this prayer of confession. He called upon God, praying "for the children of Israel Thy servants, and confess the sins of the children of Israel, which we have sinned against Thee, both I and my father's house have sinned" (Nehemiah 1:6-7). Church revitalization is the result of a humble confession.

It has troubled me as to how some pastors have attended a seminar on church revitalization and returned to their church thinking that if they remove the choir and replace it with a band, the church will turn around. Or perhaps removing the pews and setting up tables to eat on will draw a crowd. These so-called methods are dividing many churches today. This reminds of the 1960s and '70s, when some pastors were caught up in the Charismatic movement. Some claimed to have been baptized in the Holy Spirit and spoke in tongues. During those years a number of churches split.

Carefully observe Nehemiah. He did not begin rebuilding the wall with a band, nor were his actions a movement of the flesh. Nehemiah simply turned to God, humbling himself and confessing his sins and the sins of his people. Let us all remember the parable of the soils. The soils were different, and so it is with the church. If you do not understand the different soils, you will always be discouraged. Begin rebuilding the wall where the church is. Lead them gently, lovingly and firmly. It takes love and patience, but what a joy it is!

What has always been so encouraging to me is to witness what happens after a humble confession of sins. As it was with Nehemiah, God raises up a remnant, a small number of believers, who show up and assist you. Encourage your church to adopt the theme "Rebuilding the Wall" over the next five to seven years, based on Nehemiah 4:6: "So built we the wall; and all the wall was joined together unto the half thereof: for the people had a mind to work."

By being up front with the church members and everyone outside of the church — that is, the community, neighborhoods and prospects — it will be clear that your church has a goal to rebuild. This theme should be on all bulletins, newsletters, brochures and every sign. As this is being done, every member, active or inactive, should be contacted by letter, visit, phone call, and email, calling upon everyone to pray and to come to help rebuild the wall! We are told in Acts 16:9 that the Apostle Paul had a vision that appeared to him in the night. There stood a man of Macedonia saying, "Come over into Macedonia and help us." Keep this in mind: "My God shall supply all your need according to His riches in glory by Christ Jesus" (Philippians 4:19).

Rebuilding the wall of your church may seem like an impossibility, so be encouraged by Hebrews 11:34. In Hebrews 11, we find a number of names of our heroes of the faith, but do not overlook verse 34, as these were "out of weakness ... made strong." God can take your weakness and the weakness of your church and bring much glory to our Lord and Savior Jesus Christ as the wall of your church is being rebuilt!

If the remnant of God's people within the church will stand upon the Word of God, pray and exercise their faith, God will show up, manifest Himself and increase the faith of His people. At this point, the church can begin rebuilding the wall with a spirit of preparation. Nehemiah begins to exercise his faith through his prayer: "O Lord, I beseech Thee, let now

Thine ear be attentive to the prayer of Thy servant, and to the prayer of Thy servants, who desire to fear Thy name: and prosper, I pray Thee, Thy servant this day and grant him mercy in the sight of this man, for I was the king's cupbearer" (Nehemiah 1:11).

Be reminded: Everything begins with confession of sin and repentance. The psalmist confessed: "If I regard iniquity in my heart, the Lord will not hear me" (Psalm 66:18). Personal sins must be dealt with in order for the church to experience the wisdom and power of God. Be honest with God, as the psalmist was when he prayed, "Search me, O God, and know my heart, try me and know my thoughts, and see if there be any wicked way in me, and lead me in the way everlasting" (Psalm 139:23-24). We can claim God's promise: "If we confess our sins, He is faithful and just to forgive our sins, and to cleanse us from all unrighteousness" (1 John 1:9).

A complete restoration will result as the Bible comes alive. Romans 10:17 tells us: "Faith cometh by hearing, and hearing by the Word of God." From day one, the goal of the church is to have everyone under the Word. Sunday school, preaching, worship, and making Bible study the top priority will bring excitement.

In rebuilding the wall with consistency and joy, remember our purpose: "For the Son of Man is come to seek and to save that which was lost" (Luke 19:10). The Bible tells us how to achieve this goal: "Go out into the highways and hedges, and compel them to come in, that My house may be filled" (Luke 14:23). Growing a church means going after lost people — all people — every day. Once a church becomes excited about reaching the lost, it is on its way to revitalization.

When Nehemiah spoke to the remnant, reminding them of the distress they were in, how Jerusalem was lying in waste and the gates of Jerusalem were burned with fire, he said unto them, "Let us build up the wall of Jerusalem that we be no more a reproach." Those who heard him responded, "Let us rise and build" (Nehemiah 2:17-18). How will you respond?

Chapter Review: Rebuilding the Wall

Nehemiah 1:4

A Spirit of Realization
  Nehemiah 1:3

A Spirit of Consecration
  Nehemiah 1:4

A Spirit of Biblical Proposition
  Nehemiah 1:5

A Spirit of Confession
  Nehemiah 1:6-7

A Spirit of Preparation
  Nehemiah 1:11; Psalm 139:23-24; Psalm 66:18;
  Luke 19:10; Luke 14:23

A Spirit of Restoration
  Romans 10:17

A Spirit of Revitalization
  Nehemiah 2:17-18

Chapter Three

SETTING UP A DREAM TEAM

And I arose in the night, I and some few men with me: neither told I any man what my God had put in my heart to do at Jerusalem. (Nehemiah 2:12)

Here is where church revitalization excitement begins to build within the church. As it was with Nehemiah, when a church has finally realized the need to turn back to God by consecrating the remnant to Him, the steps of faith have begun to take place.

When Nehemiah received the green light to return to Jerusalem in order to rebuild the wall, notice what he realized in the latter part of verse 8: "And the king granted me, according to the good hand of my God upon me." Nehemiah understood that this foreign king, by the grace of God and by this being the will of God — he, of all people — would be able to take on a most wonderful task: to rebuild the wall of Jerusalem!

Any pastor and the remnant that is left should rejoice at the same opportunity to rebuild the wall of the church. Ephesians 5:25 tells us that "Christ loved the church and gave Himself for it." Don't you love the church? Do you not have a wonderful privilege and joy to be used of God as did Nehemiah? Christ loved the church!

Keeping this in mind, carefully watch the next steps that Nehemiah took, and apply these steps in your church. After arriving in Jerusalem and being there for three days, Nehemiah and a "few" men arose during the night and viewed the walls and the gates of Jerusalem (2:12-13). Neither the Jews, nor the priests, nor the nobles, nor the rulers nor the rest knew what Nehemiah had done. Only a few of the remnant went with him, but still they did not know what he was planning.

Upon his return from viewing Jerusalem, he then explained to them the terrible situation and challenged them: "Let us build up the wall of Jerusalem." He then told them that the hand of God was upon him and also about the king's promises. At this time they said, "Let us rise up and build." They immediately began strengthening their hands to do the great work before them (verses 17-18).

I can only imagine the excitement of the Jews when they heard the good news. Throughout the years of my ministry, I am constantly reminded how God encouraged me through His Word and how He has always been with me. Revitalization stirs the heart, brings about joy, and results in showers of blessings! I am reminded of the psalmist who asked, "Wilt thou not revive us again: that thy people may rejoice in thee?" (Psalm 85:6). I remind you of what Jesus said in Mark 9:23: "If thou canst believe all things are possible to him that believeth."

My heart is thrilled as I am reminded how God has revealed Himself to and confirmed His presence to the struggling churches in my ministry. It was in my first pastorate while attending Bible college. Here was a small church called Unity Baptist Church. It was a division from another church far, far out in the country. I was a bi-vocational pastor — actually, I was tri-vocational! I cut and styled hair part-time, was a student part-time, and I was a young pastor who was green behind the ears! I pastored and taught Sunday school, discipleship training, preached on Sunday mornings, Sunday evenings and Wednesday evenings, visited on Thursday evenings, and cut hair all day on Saturday — in addition to being a husband to a wonderful wife and having two wonderful sons. Now how could I pastor and lead this little church? There were thirty-one people present my first Sunday. Fifteen of these came in on a church bus! The church sign out front was lying on the ground with white paint plastered over the former pastor's name. What did I know about growing a church?!

One day I came across a certain book. I do not remember the name or the author of the book. I do remember the author quoting Dr. R.A. Torrey's "Prescription for a Revival." As a matter of fact, I not only wrote down the prescription, I also applied it to my ministry for each church that I pastored. Many years passed, and I came to realize that his prescription was so much like Nehemiah and what he did. I trust you will write this in your Bible and always refer to it! Dr. R.A. Torrey said this:

> *I can give a prescription that will bring a revival to any church or community or city on earth. Here it is: First, let a few Christians get thoroughly right with God themselves. This is the prime essential. If this is not done, the rest I am going to say will come to nothing. Second, let them bind themselves together in prayer groups to pray for revival until God opens the heavens and comes down. Third, let them put themselves at the disposal of God, for Him to use them as He sees fit in the winning of others to Christ. That is all … it cannot fail.*

My friend, we must be willing to do everything He said. We cannot be like the lady who asked for a recipe because it was so delicious. Instead of going by the recipe, here is what she did!

> *I didn't have potatoes, so I substituted rice,*
> *I didn't have paprika, so I used another spice.*
> *I didn't have tomato sauce, so I used tomato paste,*
> *Not a half a can, a whole can, I don't believe in waste.*
> *A friend gave me a recipe. She said you couldn't beat it.*
> *There must be something wrong with me; I couldn't even eat it!*

As a pastor who has worked with several struggling churches, I am a witness to Nehemiah's steps and to R.A. Torrey's prescription. God can revitalize any church! Unity Baptist Church, having someone like me, in less than thirty-six months added classrooms to their facilities, connected their buildings, put up a new steeple, grew to eighty-eight in average attendance with 144 in Sunday school for High Attendance Day, and the church was then ready to call its first full-time pastor.

Both Nehemiah and R.A. Torrey began with a "few" believers, and they had a plan. In order to set up a dream team, a few humble, faithful and dedicated members who desire to see the church revitalized and who will be ready to help lead and influence others must be sought out in private.

I remember becoming the pastor of West Gantt First Baptist Church. I was told that their attendance had been in steady decline for years and that there were no children, only three or four youth, one young adult couple, and that the rest were senior citizens. The members of the search committee shared their deep concerns about the possibility of one day closing down.

After accepting their call to come and help the church, I spent the first year observing the people and listening to the members, seeking out those few who would make up our dream team. Welford Crowe was the chairman of the search committee, and I discovered that everyone spoke well of this man of God. Everyone also spoke well of Fran Watson. She was a faithful, great-spirited Sunday school teacher with an outstanding reputation and whose Sunday school class was the largest in number. Jane Criswell had served on the search committee and was recognized as a prayer warrior and a great-spirited leader. Dale Johnson was a very successful business man and a faithful deacon who knew the policies, procedures and building codes. I would need his help with facility planning. He would be able to guide us with the architect, the bids and regulations. Jim Kohn was very wise with finances, and he had a gentle, kind disposition, along with a great reputation. I approached these and others who were great role models, asking them to pray about being on a dream team. I explained the process and goals we could establish. I needed those few who could be positive, patient and excited about the future of the church.

At my first meeting with our dream team, I had prepared a long list of things that needed to be done in and around the church. There were two three-story educational buildings that had not been renovated in thirty or forty years. You can imagine what we were facing! When the list was given to each member of the dream team, they were asked to take the list home, pray over it, add any additional needs they knew about, and bring everything back to our next meeting. We would discuss it and pray over it. By the end of our first meeting, we had begun establishing our needs, changes and adjustments and were ready to call in spiritual, financial and material advisors. This team's only responsibility was to dream — and dream, they did! Through the dream team's faith in God, we were able to renovate our facilities, reorganize our Sunday school structure, and develop a plan of action to pay for all the improvements over a period of time. Thank God for this dream team!

I thought I would retire from the pastorate at this church, but God had other plans. Delano McMinn, a retired director of missions, asked me to meet with a search committee from Laurel Baptist Church. This church was about to sell their property and close down. After meeting with this committee over a period of eight months, God challenged my heart. After much prayer, I accepted the call to come and help them in church revitalization. Again, a dream team was established. God provided that remnant of positive, full-of-faith believers.

This was, no doubt, my greatest challenge ever. Gertie Mullis had served as the chairman of the search committee. The other members of this committee who were involved in bringing me on as their pastor, including Gertie, Carol Marshall, Bill Heath and Linda Miller, were a few of the dedicated remnant whom God used to help revitalize the church. Here was a one-time leading church in the Greenville area that had fallen into the low thirties in Sunday school attendance. The same number of people were attending worship.

We expanded the number of those who would serve on our dream team. Faithful, positive members were added to our team. No angry, loud-mouthed pessimists would serve on this dream team. We began to establish a 20/20 vision for 2020. (This will be discussed in the next chapter.)

Everything up to this point is so positive and exciting. Now, we must understand that the devil cannot stand the church because we are the body of Christ. He does not want God to receive any glory, so he has his puppets nearby to do his bidding. We find this to be so in Nehemiah 2:19 with three men. In each ministry that I have been involved with, there have also been men like Sanballat the Horonite; and Tobia the servant, the Ammonite; and Geshem, the Arabian. Yes, the enemy will also be around.

These men will ridicule, criticize, mock and try to control you. I remember in one church after our dream team had presented its goals to the church, we were in the family life center. A certain man, a member of the church who was standing with several other men, called me across the gym floor to ask me how I expected to take on such a project. The doom-and-gloom member is always around, throwing stones and ridiculing everything. These folks will make fun of you and try to make the going rough. When I returned home, the other men who were standing with him called me to say that they all supported our dream team!

I appreciate so much Nehemiah's response when he answered those three men by saying, "The God of heaven, He will prosper us; therefore we his servants will arise and build: but ye have no portion, nor right, nor memorial in Jerusalem (Nehemiah 2:20). What was he trying to say to them? He was saying, "Get out of our way. We are going to work because God has promised to bless us!" I like what a senior pastor in our area has always told his congregation, something like this: "Get on, get off, get over or get run over!"

My friend, the dream team that is involved in the revitalization process is of utmost importance. The purpose of the dream team is to bring honor and glory to God. It is a ministry that shares the vision of the pastor and church leadership with every family concerning future plans and ministries. The entire church body will be encouraged and challenged with a renewed fellowship, through working together as a result of information, visitation and preparation. Every member and prospect will be informed of the needs and goals presented by the dream team, pastor and deacon body. The working of the dream team produces a process of informing the church, and new members, of the church's vision, growth plans and future ministries by giving everyone the opportunity to participate spiritually, physically and financially.

The God of Nehemiah is the same yesterday, today and forever. He will be with us, as He was with Nehemiah. Those in Nehemiah's day said, "Let us rise up and build." How will you respond?

Delano McMinn once challenged our church to rise up and build in four ways.

First, by going; "And the Lord said unto the servant, Go out into the highways and hedges and compel them to come in, that my house may be filled" (Luke 14:23). "Go you therefore, and teach all nations, baptizing them in the name of the Father, and of the Son, and of the Holy Spirit" (Matthew 28:19). "Say not ye, there are yet four months, and then cometh harvest? Behold, I say unto you, lift up your eyes, and look on the fields; for they are white already to harvest" (John 4:35).

Second, by giving: "Give and it shall be given unto you; good measure, pressed down, and shaken together, and running over, shall men give into your bosom. For with the same measure that ye mete withal it shall be measured to you again" (Luke 6:38). "Honor the Lord with thy substance, and with the first fruits of all thine increase:" (Proverbs 3:9). "Bring ye all the tithes into the storehouse, that there may be meat in mine house, and prove me now herewith, saith the Lord of Hosts , if I will not open you the windows of heaven and pour you out a blessing, that there shall not be room enough to receive it" (Malachi 3:10).

Third, by growing: "But grow in grace, and in the knowledge of our Lord and Savior Jesus Christ. To him be glory both now and forever. Amen" (2 Peter 3:18). "Days should speak and multitude of years should teach wisdom" (Job 32:7). "When I was a child, I spoke like a child, I thought like a child, I reasoned like a child. When I became a man, I put away childish things" (1 Corinthians 13:11). "And I, brethren, could not speak unto you as unto spiritual, but as unto carnal, even as babes in Christ. I have fed you with milk and not with meat; for hitherto ye were not able to bear it, neither yet now are ye able. For ye are yet carnal; for whereas there is among you envying, and strife, and divisions, are ye not carnal, and walk as men?" (1 Corinthians 3:1-3).

And finally, fourth, by glowing: "These who are wise will shine like the brightness of the heavens, and those who lead many to righteousness like the stars forever and ever" (Proverbs 12:3). "But the path of the just is as the shining light, that shineth more and more unto the perfect day" (Proverbs 4:18). Let your light so shine before men, that they may see your good works, and glorify your Father which is in heaven" (Matthew 5:16).

Church revitalization! This is what this book is all about. God's people responded to Nehemiah by saying, "Let us rise and build." As your dream team begins to develop a 20/20 vision, I want to personally encourage you to rise and shine!

Chapter Review: Setting Up a Dream Team

Nehemiah 2:12

Where Excitement Begins
    Ephesians 5:25; Nehemiah 2:12-13; Psalm 85:6; Mark 9:23

A Prescription for Revitalization

Choosing the Few

Expecting Opposition

Rising Up to Build

McMinn's Challenge

Rise and Shine!

Chapter Four

DEVELOPING A 20/20 VISION

And the Lord answered me, and said, Write the vision, and make it plain upon the tables, that they many run that readeth it. (Habakkuk 2:2)

There is joy in church revitalization! Yes, this is an Old Testament text, yet it is a passage of scripture that will motivate the church of our Lord Jesus Christ.

Over the nearly forty years of my ministry, this passage of scripture has been used as a spark to catch the church on fire, spiritually. As believers in Jesus Christ, we have heard Proverbs 29:18 quoted many times: "Where there is no vision, the people perish." This verse is easy to quote, but the truth is that most churches do not have a vision, nor do they have a clue about receiving a vision. For this reason, many churches are in a steady decline and have lost hope.

Nehemiah declared to his people: "For the joy of the Lord is your strength" (Nehemiah 8:10). It is my desire to help every Christian and every church to experience the joy of the Lord through church revitalization. Jesus said, "I am come that they might have life and have it more abundantly" (John 10:10). If you will simply follow the scripture throughout this chapter, you will begin experiencing joy and a fresh vision within your life and your church.

In the struggling churches where I was called to minister, I placed a banner behind the pulpit area and choir. The scripture from Habakkuk 2:2 was placed on the banner in order for every member of the church and every visitor to read it. After several weeks, the church would begin thinking more and more about the word "vision," and God would begin revealing His vision to us. There is something about this passage that would cause the church to be stirred.

As believers, we claim to believe the Bible, and we say that His words are true. If this be the case, then why are so many of our churches living in constant decline, discouragement and defeat? Why are so many pastors, deacons, leaders, and other believers living in bondage and boredom, and are beaten down? Where is the joy in the church? Where is the joy in your life? My friend, here lies the joy: It is "the joy of the Lord." Here is where you find joy and strength. It is in the Lord!

To experience this joy, there are three things that should surround your life and the life of your church. First, there should be a dream or vision. Again, I quote Proverbs 29:18: "Without a vision the people perish." How can we write a vision when there is no vision? We must dream, and have that vision from the Lord, in order to share it with others.

Where does this vision or dream come from? How does a dream become a reality? There are four ways whereby this becomes reality: First, it begins with prayer. Like Nehemiah, we must get alone with God and pray. We must be serious about God. There must be a willingness and a seriousness about giving God complete control of your life and your church.

Second, in addition to prayer, one must be in the Bible, the Word of God. We should feast on God's Word daily! Do not use the excuse, "I don't understand it." If you do not understand it, then keep reading until you do understand it! Read the Word and hear the Word through preaching and teaching.

Third, we are to receive the Word by allowing the scriptures to speak to us.

Then, fourth, act upon the Word! Exercise your faith! Yes, prayer is the key to heaven, but it is faith that unlocks the door!

Back during the 1980s, I was called to serve as pastor of Temple Baptist Church in Simpsonville, South Carolina. Soon after, we established a "dream team" and wrote our vision clearly. We stood on Habakkuk 2:2. In the beginning of my ministry there, we only had some $25,000 on hand in our bank account. We were landlocked, with only about six inches of property along the side of our property. There were a few parking spaces in front of our facility and a few behind our building. The entire educational facility needed renovating.

I encouraged the church to step out on faith — just a little faith — and have an architect draw up a preliminary plan for renovations. Preliminary plans are not expensive. Immediately, some began to say that we did not have the income needed to renovate. This was true; however, all I was seeking was a plan to place in our vestibule and welcome center for everyone to see and read. All it took was a plan that was framed and placed on two easels. That was all!

Jesus said, "If ye have faith as a grain of mustard seed, ye might say unto this sycamine tree, Be thou plucked up by the root; and be thou planted in the sea; and it should obey you" (Luke 17:6). After much prayer, we took the words of our Lord from Habakkuk 2:2 and applied them to our church. We read the Word, heard the Word, received the Word and acted upon the Word. Within twelve months, our deacons and members were asking excitedly, "When can we begin? Why can't we get started?"

Another dream or vision we had written down was for us to purchase property near our church. Where was the faith? I asked each deacon to go to every house on our block and simply make a request: If the owner were ever to consider selling their property, would they please give our church the first opportunity to make the purchase? Again, there were those of our membership who stated that we did not have the money to purchase all of these houses, and they were correct. We did not have the money available. My response was, "It is true." Neither did the homeowners want to sell their property, but — who knows — after much prayer, one day they may sell to us! Well, here it is now, 2016, and every house on the entire block and all the other property belongs to Temple Baptist Church! Glory to God! My friend, if this does not ring your bell, your clapper is broken! It all began with a dream!

Not only should there be a dream, we must realize there must also be a dedication. Galatians 6:9 states: "And let us not be weary in well doing; for in due season we shall reap, if we faint not." Second Timothy 2:2 tells us to "commit thou to faithful men, who shall be able to teach others also." We must remain faithful to God's Word by daily searching the scriptures, and we must remain faithful to prayer, to the church and to serving our God. Some are always quitting or on the verge of quitting! There must be dedication.

Along with our dream and our dedication, there must be a determination. Habakkuk 2:3 tells us: "For the vision is yet for an appointed time, but at the end it shall speak, and not lie; though it tarry, wait for it; because it will surely come, it will not tarry." Do not look back and live in the past. Be determined that the best days for your church are ahead and not in the past. The Apostle Paul said it best: "Brethren, I count not myself to have apprehended; but this one thing I do, forgetting those things which are behind, and reaching forth unto those things which are before, I press forward toward the mark for the prize of the high calling of God in Christ Jesus" (Philippians 3:14).

Be determined to reach your goals, more goals and new goals until Jesus comes again! Forget those things in your past that are now hindering you and your church. Your sins are under the blood of Jesus, so forget the past, your failures, your disappointments, your heartbreaks and victories. Do not live in the past! Press on! Press toward the mark — that which God has placed upon your heart through prayer and through His Word. Your best days are ahead! Someone once said, "God put the worms out there for the birds, but the birds must be determined to go get them!" This is what church revitalization is all about. You can take your mountain, but if you remain as you are, being fearful and not exercising your faith in God's Word, you will fail. Do not grow weary in well doing, for in due season you shall reap if you faint not. Dream on!

When we dream, we must be dedicated and determined, and we must have a destiny. The Apostle Paul tells us there is a "prize" before us. What is the prize? There are actually many prizes for those who follow Christ. Consider these: There is forgiveness of sins, eternal life, the abundant life, the anointing, the power of God, His grace and mercy, the ability to see through His eyes and to have a dream, a vision, to see the goals before us and to have His promises that He will never leave us or forsake us, and that He will supply all our needs according to His riches in glory in Christ Jesus. Through Christ we are able to see through His eyes what others cannot see.

Allow me now to share just two examples of churches that were about to close their doors. On the following pages, you will see where dream teams were established and how they set up their 20/20 vision for the future.

The first 20/20 vision is from Laurel Baptist Church in Greenville, South Carolina. This was once a very successful church that had some 500-plus in attendance back in the 1970s. Their attendance in 2011 had fallen to around thirty in worship attendance and in Sunday school. From my understanding, there had been only one baptism during the previous five years. There were all kinds of facilities on the property, but they were in need of much repair. Their offering averaged around $1,100 per week, and their total missions offering was around $1,800 per year. Thousands of dollars would be needed to renovate the facilities. (More about this church will be shared in another chapter.)

For anyone or any church that feels as though you have hit rock bottom, I ask you to examine closely the 20/20 vision for Laurel Baptist Church. After reviewing this, begin establishing your own 20/20 vision as God directs you and your dream team.

Notice the vision is divided into three areas. First, there is a spiritual vision. Matthew 6:33 instructs us to "seek ye first the kingdom of God, and His righteousness and these things shall be added unto you." Many churches continue in a decline because their priorities are either backward or mixed up. The spiritual vision must be first. Secondly, there is a material vision. No, you cannot do everything on your list at once; but everything needs to be written down, and then, one by one, seek to reach your goal. Third is a financial vision. When your members begin to examine the spiritual and the material vision, they will be much more enthused about setting up their financial vision. Remember, both of these churches about whom I am sharing with you were about to close their doors!

Hosannah Baptist Church is an African-American church located in McCormick, South Carolina. When I was made aware of this church, my wife and I were on a vacation at Hickory Knob State Park. There I met Dean Freeman, who was employed with Savannah Lakes. In a conversation with Dean, I asked about an old, small white building near the park. He informed me that it was a church with only about twelve members attending. One family in this little church had a wreck in Atlanta, Georgia, killing the son and paralyzing the father from his chest down. Dean asked me to please pray for Hosannah Baptist Church. Right then and there, we prayed. Dean also informed me that he was raised, taught, saved and baptized as a result of the ministry of the church. He was no longer a member of this church, but his heart was broken over its current condition.

I asked Dean if he could give me the name of the family that had suffered so much, which he did. Alice Crawford was the wife of the paralyzed man and the mother of the son who was killed in the accident. I called Alice and asked if I could meet with her and the other members of the church as soon as possible. Eventually, we met together and I asked if they would allow me to place a sign in front of the church with the name of the church and times of the services each week and also to install a banner above the pulpit with the words from Habakkuk 2:2. They agreed, and from that day forward, we have grown together in the Lord. This was thirteen years ago! We are still trying to complete a new worship center. I have preached funerals for some of the members there. They now have a wonderful pastor, Rev. Clyde Cannon. I truly love these dear people.

This church set up their dream team and established a 20/20 vision that has excited the congregation, the community and other churches, as well — because everyone thought that the church was going to close.

Here are two churches that set up a 20/20 vision. Begin with your dream team. Write your vision. Dream on!

Below you will find a simple example of a 20/20 vision for you to glean. Remember, here was a church at rock bottom, about to close its doors.

Begin praying. Be dedicated and determined. Have a destiny. What do you hope to see this week … this month … this year? What about five years from now or ten or twenty years from now? What do you hope and trust to experience in your church? Dream on!

You have read the Word and heard the Word. Now, will you receive the word and act upon the Word?

A 20/20 Vision for 2020

Laurel Baptist Church

(This church was about six months away from closing its doors)

Where there is no vision, the people perish. (Proverbs 29:18)

And the Lord answered me, and said, "Write the vision, and make it plain upon tables, that he may run that readeth it." (Habakkuk 2:2)

For the vision is yet for an appointed time, but at the end it shall speak, and not lie: though it tarry, wait for it; because it will surely come, it will not tarry. (Habakkuk 2:3)

Our Spiritual Vision

The Word of God #1

Develop strong spiritual leaders

Emphasis on:

    A strong Sunday school

    Small groups

    Bible school

    Seminars and retreats teaching the Word of God

Develop and expand the ACTS ministry, encouraging every believer to discover their spiritual gifts

Develop plans to strongly emphasize a children's ministry (priority)

Develop leaders for a new and growing AWANA ministry

Plan and develop children's and youth retreats, with emphasis on teaching the Bible, winning them to Christ, and maturing them in the Lord

Develop, train and encourage our people to be friendly, welcoming and serving

Develop a serious, consistent FAITH ministry to train our members how to become soul winners

Send out missionaries (career and short-term) all around the world, beginning here at home

Our Material Vision

Completion of sound and video system upgrades

Finish remodeling of our children's department

Cemetery planning and improvements

Welcome center improvements

Enlarge pulpit and altar area

Third-floor HVAC and bathroom upgrades

Prepare basement for a new mission ministry

Playground construction (with fencing, benches, tables)

Landscaping and building exterior upgrades

Digital monument sign in front of church

Parking lot resurfacing and restriping

Install additional ceiling insulation in sanctuary and third floor

Gym floor, backboards, scoreboard and bathrooms

New roof, drains and HVAC on children's wing

New roof on family life center

Carport for bus and van

Estimated total cost: $382,000-$477,000

Future: Purchase property for a new church start

Our Financial Vision

— To encourage tithing

— To provide special offering opportunities

— To motivate giving through spiritual growth

— To promote yearly "The Chest of Joash"

— To communicate biblically the benefits of giving

— To establish church budgets with wisdom, balance and faith to challenge God's people

— To increase our mission giving to the Greenville Baptist Association, the Cooperative Program and other Southern Baptist causes

— Educate and help members with wills, CDs and other gifts with help from the Baptist Foundation

— Develop a thirty-six-month "Rebuilding the Wall" campaign to allow each member to participate and give on a monthly basis to accomplish our vision — "Not Equal Giving, but Equal Sacrifice"

Chapter Review: Developing a 20/20 Vision

Habakkuk 2:2-3

There is joy in church revitalization
    Proverbs 29:18; Nehemiah 8:10; John 10:10

There are 4 things that should surround your church

There are 4 ways for this to become a reality
    Luke 17:6

Two examples to help develop a 20/20 vision
    Habakkuk 2:3
    Hosannah Baptist Church
    Laurel Baptist Church

Chapter Five

ESTABLISHING A CHURCH GROWTH CALENDAR

For the Son of Man is come to seek and to save that which was lost. (Luke 19:10)

Look closely at this verse of scripture from Luke 19:10. As Christians, we say that we believe the Bible. We profess Jesus as Savior and Lord and believe that He has given to us the Great Commission in Matthew 28:18-20: "All power is given unto me in heaven and in earth. Go ye therefore, and teach all nations, baptizing them in the name of the Father, and of the Son, and of the Holy Ghost; teaching them to observe all things whatsoever I have commanded you; and lo, I am with you always, even unto the end of the world. Amen."

If we truly believe this, then why are there so few Christians "going," "teaching," and "baptizing?" It has amazed me over the years as to how few pastors, deacons, directors, teachers and members are ever involved in "going" outside the stained glass windows of our churches, sharing the gospel or even compelling others to come into God's house that His house may be filled. We have "hired" a preacher, and we expect him to grow our church. Many church members are involved in so many good activities but are never involved in the outreach ministry of the church.

I was one of those members while serving as a Sunday school teacher, deacon, choir member and on numerous committees. One day when I was in my mid-twenties, sitting in a worship service, the Holy Spirit began to convict me while my pastor was preaching. I came to realize that I had never actually led anyone to Jesus Christ. I was involved in outreach but never had personally led anyone to Christ. As of that Sunday, it became my desire to learn how to lead someone to Jesus Christ.

In those days, we simply learned the "Romans Road" as our witnessing tool. Later, we learned how to share our faith through Christian Witness Training, and then through FAITH Training. All of these tools were, and are, excellent in teaching believers how to become soul winners.

I had been raised in a Southern Baptist Church that taught and expected the staff and deacons to be involved in the outreach ministry of the church. We had weekly visitation nights scheduled. On Saturdays, there was a weekly radio station where our church shared the gospel through preaching, testimonies and singing. Each month there was a Sunday afternoon designated for a jail service in our small town. The pastor, deacons and others shared the gospel with the prisoners. I thank my God for these wonderful days in training under such great men and women of God!

Upon entering the ministry and becoming a pastor, I was shocked to see how many deacons, teachers and even church staff members did not have a clue as to how to lead a lost soul to Christ. I remember in my first church, at an invitation, several came forward to receive Christ. I turned to several leaders, teachers, deacons and others to go over the plan of salvation with these who had come forward. Some stated they were not sure what to say. Some shared with me later that this was a scary thing to go through because they were not sure if they were giving the right information.

God gave me a wonderful opportunity to serve on an ordination council years ago. The person being ordained had been serving as a music director, and he believed God was calling him to preach. This young man had graduated from one of our Baptist colleges and also from a Presbyterian seminary. A question was asked by a retired senior professor from that same Baptist college. Here is what he asked the young man being ordained: "If you preached one Sunday and after the services someone came to you and asked, 'What must I do to be saved?' how would you respond? What answer would you give?" The young man responded by saying, "Put your trust in Jesus." The old professor continued by saying, "What do you mean by trusting in Jesus? Can you give us some scripture as to how he would trust in Jesus?" This young man stated that he could not give the scripture and that he would have to look it up. To that, the old professor said, "Son, before you ever pastor and stand behind the pulpit to preach, the first thing you should know is how to lead a soul to Christ." He continued by saying to the young man that he could not believe that he had graduated from two Christian institutions and had never been taught how to lead someone to Christ!

My friend, this describes most of our churches today. Very little do we hear about the Great Commission in our day. Very few believers are involved in the outreach ministry of the church. I also remember a young lady in her thirties who came forward to receive Christ. There was a faithful young lady, also in her thirties, who was nearby, and she was a very faithful Sunday school teacher. I asked this teacher to counsel the one who had come forward. The young Sunday school teacher took this young convert aside, and they both sat on the front seat of our worship center. They both just sat there. At the end of the service, I approached the young teacher and asked if she shared the scripture with the new convert. The teacher responded by saying, "Preacher, I know I am saved, but I just do not know what to say to her."

I am not writing this to belittle any one of these people. There was a time when I served actively in the church with no understanding about leading someone through the scriptures for salvation.

Jesus came to seek and to save that which was lost! This is what the church is all about! We can have an Easter egg hunt, a church party, an eating meeting or a Super Bowl party, and people will come out — temporarily, until next year or at the next whoopee!

Remember, this chapter is about establishing a church growth calendar! For a church to be revitalized, we must understand the importance of this task. We all must admit that little to nothing on most of our church calendars has anything to do with soul winning or outreach outside of our church rolls. Most people are interested in dropping people from the rolls of our churches and classes, without even making a visit. We would rather have 100 percent of five or six members present than to enroll lost people in our Sunday school classes in order to win them to Jesus.

Years ago, my wife and I were on vacation and we visited a certain church. We were taken to a class where there was a teacher and one class member. The teacher shared with us that she would rather have one person present who would be willing to listen than to have a class full who would not listen. I thought to myself that she has reached her goal.

In Matthew 18:14, Jesus tells us, "Even so it is not the will of your Father which is in heaven that one of these little ones should perish." If Jesus is come to seek and to save that which was lost, should we not make this our priority in church revitalization? When I entered the ministry and became a pastor, I realized how few there would be who would be participating in outreach. Because of this truth, I began seeking ways to involve the church in outreach. One of these was by establishing a church growth calendar.

In January 1983, I became a full-time pastor of one of the most wonderful churches in Anderson, South Carolina. This, no doubt, was one of my most exciting ministries. I was young and motivated. Looking back, I may have been like a bull in a china shop! My 1983 calendar was all prepared and well organized — I thought! To my surprise, the church already had their calendar and, believe me, it was filled to capacity! The main problem was there was no room for evangelism and outreach. I had plans to take the children on a retreat in May, and we had some twenty-five to thirty children ready to go. However, the church van had already been scheduled for a number of meals for the adults. In addition, no one wanted to assist or be chaperones! Here we were, with reservations made, and no way to get there! I had to seek transportation from different sources and with only two adults going — the pastor and his wife!

We scheduled a church growth crusade during the month of May with evangelist Aubert Rose. We had a special night planned for each service including a "pack-a-pew" night. For the first service, Aubert handed me a bulletin and he asked me to look on the back of it. Can you believe this: On the back of that bulletin was a list of all the softball games that were to be played during the month, including during our church growth crusade week!

What did I learn from this? I learned that this is one of the reasons our churches are in such a mess. Our priorities are all out of order. We have become no more than a social club. For me, 1983 became the year of learning. I had to learn how to be patient and wise in making changes and prudent in my planning. Before 1984 rolled around, I not only had my calendar of events ready, but I had also met with my staff, deacons and key leaders, involving them in the planning process and explaining that evangelism and outreach must be our top priority. Most everyone was on board and working together during that year.

In establishing our church calendar, here are some things we did that helped us involve more people in outreach. I pray that this will help you and your church, as well.

First and foremost, Monday night was cleared for evangelism and outreach. We asked that nothing else be planned on that night unless it was an emergency. This had to be top priority. No one could ever say that the preacher did not visit! As a result of this decision by the church, my ministry and this church remained motivated all the while I was there! You should understand that this church was a Southern Baptist church. This new calendar meant that our new church year would begin in September. (In the 1980s the church year began in October).

For the following, let us assume that the church year starts in

September. I want to share some special dates that will challenge and encourage your membership in reaching more people for Christ. These dates will boost your attendance, and more souls will be saved.

As a pastor, I have discovered that the months of January and February are not only cold, but are also are great months to spend time in planning your calendar. June, July and August, likewise, are great months to prepare for the new church year that will start in September. In August, with the church calendar prepared, a meeting of all leaders should take place in order to pray and to promote the special days and to organize for outreach.

Since the first Sunday in September is a national holiday weekend, this is an opportunity to promote a "No Absentee Day" in Sunday school for the second Sunday in September. What is the goal? To have no absentees in Sunday school. (Yes, there will always be some absentees, but your Sunday school and worship attendance will increase.)

Years ago, I read a book by Dr. Jack Hyles, an Independent Baptist pastor from Hammond, Indiana. In his book there was an example of a letter that he would send out to every person possible in promoting this special day. I have used this many times over the years and it helps so much. In his book, he encourages others to use it, so allow me to pass it on. (I adjusted the letter to fit our church.)

September 4, 2012

My Dear Friend,

We are cerxainly hoping xhax you can be in Sunday school xhis nexx Sunday ax Laurel Bapxisx Church. Since school has sxarxed and also due xo xhe facx xhax many of our people have been sick laxely, several have been absenx xhe lasx few Sundays. We wanx xo sxarx xhis new church year, xhanksgiving and Chrisxmas season off righx wixh a big boom in axxendance xhis Sunday. Plan now xo be in your place. Bring all of xhe children and lex's go over xhe xop for xhe Lord Jesus.

2012 has been a good year for xhe Laurel Bapxisx Church. We are hoping xhax xhe same xhing can be said ax xhe end of 2013.

By xhe way, I guess xhax by now you are wondering why we have lefx oux all of xhe "T's" in xhis lexxer. The reason is that we have been having absent "T's" lately, and we just didn't have enough to use in this letter.

Don't be an ABSENTEE this Sunday!

Sincerely,
Your Pastor

In planning your church calendar, remember that the second Sunday of the new church year (September) is "No Absentee Day."

October is a great month to promote a "Soul Winning Commitment Sunday." The first Sunday in October is a good time to preach on soul winning, with the emphasis on calling believers to become soul winners for Christ. A FAITH training class should always be available for the purpose of teaching those who want to learn the plan of salvation and how to share the gospel.

November has been a most successful month in reaching the family. The Sunday before Thanksgiving is a day when most people are at home. This is an excellent month to put emphasis on the family. On the Sunday before Thanksgiving, we have always called this "Family Day." Our goal has been to encourage everyone to have their entire family in Sunday school and worship. Many times, an old-fashioned covered dish lunch would be planned. Special guests, singers, preachers and other guests have made this a very joyful occasion over the years. The family and Thanksgiving emphases complement one another.

The month of December is always a special time for all believers as we celebrate the birth of our Lord Jesus Christ. The music ministries, missions emphasis and all the other activities involved in worshipping our Lord make this a joyous occasion within itself. Celebrate Christmas! Make much of Christ!

In many churches, January is known generally as a let-down month. Christmas is over, the weather is cold and many people become depressed; therefore, many may not be seen for weeks or even months. This should never be the case! January can be an encouraging month, as well. Dr. Harold Hunter once suggested to me that I should schedule a "Saints Memorial Day" on the first Sunday in January. He went on to say that when Christmas is over, most churches never plan anything in January. I took his advice. Before the end of December, we gather all the names of those of our membership who have passed away during the year. We have those within our church who will call and send out letters to their family members inviting them to come for our Saints Memorial Day. We let the family members know that it is our desire to honor their deceased family member and to pray for their family. We want the family members to know that we care, and this service will show our love for them.

Remember our text: "The Son of Man is come to seek and to save that which was lost." Our special emphasis each month is to compel others to be in God's house. Their faith will come by hearing, and hearing by the Word of God. We seek to carry out the Great Commission by having these special days!

On the Saturday before the last Sunday in January, we always have a men's breakfast, either at our church or at a restaurant. All of our active men are asked to purchase a ticket for this breakfast for $8. They are also challenged to purchase a ticket for the purpose of inviting prospects, the lost, the backslidden and others to be their guests at this special breakfast. We also invite someone to come and be our guest speaker who has a personal testimony and a message sharing the gospel of our Lord Jesus. We usually have some eighty to 100 men present. We then invite each and every one to come and be present the following day, Sunday, as we have planned a service called "Men's Day" to reach the men with the gospel. This is a wonderful way to begin the new year! When you reach the men, you usually reach the entire family!

In February, you should do the same for the ladies. One Saturday, a brunch or breakfast is prepared. Tickets are available for all ladies of the church and for the prospects and guests they would like to invite. Keep in mind that the goal is not simply to have a breakfast, but to have everyone hear the gospel from the guest speaker and give them the opportunity to receive Christ as savior.

You will discover that March, April or May are good months to have either a revival or a church revitalization crusade. March is also a good month, around the last Sunday, to have a youth day. Again, your goal is to reach others for Christ by planning special events, guest speakers and testimonies. Do all you can during the entire month to reach out to other youth and to encourage the growth in your own congregation.

In April, and of course (sometimes in March), we are reminded of the resurrection as we all celebrate Easter. Make much of the resurrection through the music ministries of the church. This should always be a time of celebration for believers. Preach the Word and magnify the name of Christ through worship and singing!

The month of May is an exciting month, as well. There are four events that usually take place in my pastorate. First, we declare May to be "Ministry Month and ACTS — A Church That Serves!" We spend the entire month encouraging all of our members to sign up for service. Every member has this opportunity. We have survey sheets and opportunities for service available for all to find their place of ministry. Second, we put emphasis on Mother's Day by encouraging all family members to be present in Sunday school and worship to honor their mothers. What greater way can we honor them than by being present with them in the house of God! Third, on one Sunday in May, we plan for a senior citizen day. These people are recognized, and expressions of thanks are given to these dear ones. We want everyone to know how important each person is in the kingdom of God. There is no generation gap in God's family. Every believer is important in God's eyes, and every believer is useful in His kingdom's work. Fourth, homecoming is also promoted in May through letters, invitations and adequate preparations. Crowds will come if something is promoted well. Yes, May is an exciting month for the church.

As we enter the months of June and July, many churches fail to plan. Remember, God is not on vacation. Do not go through a period of depression during these days of vacation. Make the most of it and enjoy the activities.

In June, make much of Father's Day! Encourage all fathers and grandfathers to be present for this special occasion. Invite all family members to be in church with their fathers on this Lord's Day. This is a wonderful way to honor our fathers by being in God's house together. Also, make much of Vacation Bible School by doing everything possible to reach more children! Plan a special children's day. Anyone who tells you that, because children do not bring in tithes and offerings, they are not concerned about children, that person fails to understand what Jesus said about children! He said to "suffer little children and forbid them not to come unto me, for of such is the Kingdom of heaven" (Matthew 19:14). I have discovered over the years that this ministry is the most overlooked ministry. The one who only thinks about money should meet Wayne and Debbie Faglier; Barry, Donnie, Karen and Gary Callaway; Floyd Brooks; Noble Drake; Connie, Debbie and David Smith; and many other children I know who began attending church where I have served over the years. They are children who came to know Christ through our children's ministries. Today they have parents and grandparents who also were saved and who are now serving our Lord in different areas of ministry and who give of their tithes and offerings. Make the children's ministry a top priority in the church. Much joy comes through the children!

July is a great time to reach others. Do not allow Satan to discourage you during this time of year. Plan for this month, as well. Make it exciting! I remember in my first full-time church where I pastored, the month of July was near. My members began telling me of the McCullough and McMullan families. These two families would always go to the beach every July 4th weekend and be gone the entire week. When these two families left for vacation, they would always take at least seventy-five members with them. As soon as I heard this as a young pastor, I was immediately discouraged. Attendance would be down in Sunday school and worship. I could only imagine what our Sunday evening service would look like. As I prayed over this, God laid it upon my heart to make special plans for that weekend. I began to announce that all who would be in town on that Sunday were to bring an old-fashioned covered dish lunch and invite all their relatives, friends, and neighbors for spiritual and physical food. I asked for everyone to bring their best cooking. I shared with them that we would have special guests and singers, and we were going to have an exciting July 4th weekend in the Lord. I decided I was not going to have a depressed weekend; instead, it would be an exciting time in the Lord with food — spiritual and physical — fun and fellowship. When word began to travel around the community, the seventy-five family members and their friends decided to wait until our July 4th celebration was over and then they would travel to the beach! Glory to God! What a great day in the Lord it was. You cannot imagine the turnout of people on that day!

My friend, church revitalization is such a joy if our priorities are in order and our goal of reaching souls is first and foremost. Consider Jesus in Luke 10:17-21. I am sure Jesus rejoiced many times in His life, however, the only time we read of His rejoicing is found in this text. It was after He had sent out the seventy laborers for God's harvest. After the seventy returned, they did so with joy, saying, "Lord, even the devils are subject unto us through Thy name." What was happening here? Souls were being saved! Many were turning to Christ. Do you get the picture? Jesus was rejoicing over this good news!

Joy can return to your church! Lift up your heads and look unto the fields. They are already white with harvest. Begin now establishing your church calendar. Begin now reaching others for Christ. Church revitalization can be a reality. Simply love Jesus and love souls!

Chapter Review: Establishing a Church Growth Calendar

Luke 19:10

What we profess

What we practice

What we should pursue

What should be our priority?

Chapter Six

DISSOLVING SPIRITUAL BLOOD CLOTS (PART 1)

God is our refuge and strength, a very present help in trouble. (Psalm 46:1)

Tommy Hamlett came home one day with his leg swollen. After several days the swelling had gotten worse and was very red. He went to the emergency room, where they did an ultrasound and, as a result, discovered he had a large blood clot in his leg. The doctor ordered a CT scan about a week later to check his lungs and discovered that he had a blood clot in his lungs, also. He was then put on Xarelto, which is a blood thinner to dissolve his blood clot. He could be on this medicine at least nine to twelve months, and perhaps for the rest of his life. The reports that he has received thus far have been so good and encouraging.

When Tommy began to recognize the swelling of the leg and the redness in that area, he took action and made his way to see a doctor as soon as possible. The psalmist tells us: "God is our refuge and strength, a very present help in trouble." God is our Great Physician, and He tells us: "Call unto me, and I will answer thee, and shew thee great and might things, which thou knowest not" (Jeremiah 33:3).

Before a church can be revitalized, the members must realize and recognize that spiritual blood clots are the cause of spiritual strokes. The church should immediately go to our Great Physician and seek His help in this time of need. He has the answers to our problems, and He will help. He loves the church because we are His body. He cares, and will provide for our needs. On the following pages, I want to share with you what God has shown me over the years through some of the churches where I have been able to serve. As a result of working with these churches, I have learned to experience God and to see His hand work in my life, causing me not only to experience God, but also the joy in church revitalization.

First of all, I begin with my home church in Thomson, Georgia. This is a typical Baptist church. It would be called a very conservative church, where I learned the Bible, learned that Jesus Christ, being the Son of God, died for our sins, was buried and arose from the grave. Here is where I learned the fundamentals of the faith. Not only did I learn the fundamentals, I also was taught, not by man, but by the Holy Spirit, through the preaching of God's Word, which pointed out spiritual blood clots. As a young boy growing up in and around the church, I witnessed the effects of these blood clots. These lessons helped me so much over the years to recognize the blood clots and how to dissolve them — not by myself — but with the help of God.

I learned in this church about the "Killer B's"(spiritual blood clots), and they are Business meetings, Bylaws, Buildings and Budgets. If you want to truly understand how to revitalize your church, look carefully at these four areas. After examining these areas, take the spiritual blood clots to the Lord, and He will give your church the correct medicine to deal with much of your problem.

Let us begin with business meetings. While growing up in the church, I learned to despise business meetings! I realize these are necessary at times and the business of the church must be handled. Having been in a church for nearly sixty-seven years, I submit to you that this "Killer B" is the number-one reason why many of our churches have lost so many young adults, teenagers and children from our church rolls.

In my home church, we had our business meetings on the first Sunday of each month following our morning worship services. We would ask all guests if they would like to leave or remain for our business session. I personally wanted them to leave, because if they remained, those guests would never return. When this meeting began, we all knew what was coming! There would be a call to order. Next, there would be a reading of the minutes, a time of approval, a discussion of old minutes, reports, and, finally, a discussion of new business. In between all of this, we all knew who would be standing in front of the church giving his opinion, and then all the debating would occur. Everyone in the church knew what would happen, and we could hardly worship during the morning service because of the soon-to-be business meeting.

Whenever I was called to help revitalize a church, I always asked about their business meetings. Before accepting the call, I asked to change the way business meetings were held. The recommendations were simple, and they solved many blood clots! I would recommend that our meetings be held when our visitors would not be present (as they would be on Sunday mornings) and to cut out the number of business meetings by having them quarterly, biannually or even once a year unless something pressing needed to be brought to our attention. We also would ask the membership to bring no surprises to the church without first having the pastor and deacons discuss the matter. If and when a recommendation is made, a motion would be made on Sunday morning. If anyone had a question concerning the matter, the member or members could meet with the deacon, deacons, or ministry team on the following Wednesday evening. Everyone would have all week to ask questions. Then, on the next Sunday, we would simply vote on an approval or disapproval. No questions would be asked on this day. Why? This keeps down controversy, debate and arguments from being on the church floor in front of children, youth and visitors. Every church I have served that made this change immediately had a change in spirit, and members were encouraged and excited because it kept down so much controversy.

Why do we have business meetings only to have such boring reports? Why do we who are Baptists have someone stand up and report that certain members have united with another church, then ask the congregation to approve sending their church letter when they have already left and united elsewhere? Why do we announce this and at the same time discourage our people who are still with us and who remain faithful? Business meetings can be "Killer B's"!

The next "Killer B" is bylaws. Most bylaws are antiquated and confusing. In my home church, there was a member who would have his copy of the bylaws in his back pocket at our business meetings. He was able to quote page 3, article 4 and paragraph 2! He kept our church in a frenzy every month. I have discovered that in most every church there is a "bylaw man." He can quote the bylaws, but not very much scripture. He never comes for weekly visitation, Sunday school or prayer meeting, and he usually majors on the negative. There, my friend, is a blood clot!

A third "Killer B" is buildings. These, too, are needed, but if we're not careful, the building can be worshipped. A church can be "building mindful" and become no heavenly good. God's Word tells us to compel others to come in that the Master's house may be filled. When a church is more interested in having temple police than reaching the lost, there you will find a major blood clot. What good is it to have a spic-and-span building if the rooms are empty? What good is it to have everyone march around like wooden soldiers or like the "frozen chosen?" We should remember that lost people may be drunks, dirty or foul-mouthed. These are the people who need Christ! The church is not to be a museum, but a place of worship where dirty, lost sinners may come and be saved!

Don't get me wrong. We should care for God's house and teach others to respect the house of God, but it is not by having the temple police directing the lost and little lambs, causing them to be in bondage!

The fourth "Killer B" is budget. Examine your weak spots in the church — say, the children's ministry, youth ministry or evangelism ministry — and then compare the budget amount available for beautiful buildings, frolics and pleasure rides. A balanced budget is not always determined by income and expenses. Rather, how is the budget balanced with regard to ministries? Remember, in most churches there are very few children and youth. They do not have the income that adults have, nor do most children and youth have parents who care if their children or youth attend church or not. You and I are the only spiritual parents they have! Pray for a real "balanced" budget!

A second church where God taught me valuable lessons was in Vanna, Georgia. I had a wife and two young sons. I had enrolled in a Bible college. Having so little money, I could only take an Old and New Testament survey course while working at a barber/style shop in Royston. Attending school the first half of each day gave me the opportunity to work the second half of the day. My wife and I were in our late twenties, and my sons were ages six and three. On top of all of this, Unity Baptist Church in Vanna asked me to come and serve as their bi-vocational pastor. After much prayer, I was both humbled and excited about the challenge. Before I entered the ministry and moved to attend school, my Sunday school class back home was larger than the church that called me as pastor. At Unity Church, there were approximately thirty-one people attending Sunday school, with fifteen of them being children who were picked up by our church bus and brought in from five miles away.

Where were the blood clots? There were so many! First, the church was located five miles from Royston. If someone were to stand on the front porch of the little church building and scream, no one would hear them because they were too far away from any houses. From where would we draw people? The church sign, made out of wood, was lying on the ground with the former pastor's name covered up with white paint. Unity Baptist Church was a split from another church miles away. This was another blood clot. The church gave me $100 per week, and I preached Sunday morning and Sunday evening, taught a new Sunday school class and also taught in discipleship training. I also led in prayer services on Wednesday evening, with Bible study. Thursday evenings, after working all day, we had our weekly visitation. There were only four or five Sunday school classes. (Hang on everyone, for it gets even better!) Our pianist was a young teenager. She only knew four or five songs, so we were limited to those at every service! We did have five wonderful deacons. I was so blessed to have had the opportunity to begin my ministry there, but blood clots were everywhere!

After I became pastor, the fall season arrived. The church already had plans to have a Halloween carnival at the church. What a way to start a ministry! I had never taken part in any Halloween carnival in my home church. This was a no-no. My wife and I decided to weather the storm after sharing with the congregation that I had strong convictions against it. They laughed it off, saying it was all in fun. They asked me to be in the dunking booth, but I refused, again sharing my convictions. On the night of the carnival, I arrived at the church. Children, youth and parents were everywhere! The entire Sunday school area was decorated as a haunted house. There was even a casket in one of the classrooms! Children and youth were running throughout the church and screaming at the top of their lungs!

Talk about blood clots! They were everywhere. As soon as that week passed, I sat down with my deacons and shared my convictions and plans to change things for the following year. I suggested we change our Halloween carnival from exalting witches and evil to a fall festival glorifying our Lord Jesus Christ. If this church was serious about moving forward, this was one blood clot that had to be dissolved. It was, and God blessed the church because of that decision.

In our first revival, Dr. Raymond Wilson, pastor of Sardis Baptist Church, was invited to be our guest preacher. I will never forget his first sermon. He began by preaching about reconciliation. He shared with the church that before revival can ever take place, a church must first deal with unconfessed sin. He knew this church was a split from another church and that the desire to forgive and to be reconciled must take place. He was so correct. This was a spiritual blood clot that had to be dealt with. I realized this might not happen overnight, but I believed it would happen. We would have to allow the Holy Spirit to convict, convince and challenge His people.

Yes, blood clots were everywhere, but through the preaching of God's Word, the convicting power of the Holy Spirit, and loving the lost and backslidden, God blessed that little church! For three years I ministered there while attending Bible college, enjoying life with my precious wife, two young boys and a recently born precious young daughter, with a church salary of only $125, and still cutting and styling hair. After three years, I was called to my first full-time church.

What about the blood clots? After those three years, we were averaging eighty-eight in Sunday school with a high attendance of 144. We installed a steeple, put up a new sign, painted and remodeled the facilities, and added seven new classrooms — all without going into debt! All of my schooling was paid for, and I was able to purchase new furniture for the house I would be moving into. My friend, any church can be revitalized if only we will turn to our Great Physician!

A third church that was revitalized was Union Baptist Church in Iva, South Carolina. Iva had a population then of 1,360 and a zip code of E-I-E-I-O! What a blessing this was! But where were the blood clots? Here was a church that averaged 144 in Sunday school. The pastor had retired after thirty-three years of service. This, no doubt, was my most exciting ministry over the years. I love those dear people!

Let's look closely at the spiritual blood clots. First, it was me! The pastor who had just retired was a graduate of Anderson College, and he received his master's degree from one of our Southern Baptist seminaries. The church had two school principals who were members and several fine school teachers, as well. A number of our members were business men and women who were highly educated, and then there was little ol' me! I had not received even an associate degree after three years of schooling. What was I doing at this church? Why would they want me? When I preached my first sermon, it was entitled, "The Old-Time Religion." I wanted the people to know that even though I was young, I believed the "old book," the old-time gospel and the fundamentals of the Christian faith. I believed the Bible, and I believed the cover of the Bible. It was, and it is, God's Holy Word! Can you believe it? I received 100 percent of the vote that day! Glory to God!

Now let's look at the other blood clots! Within this church there were a great number of senior men, but there were hardly any young men who attended Bible study or worship. There were only two young children in the nursery, and there was one young ladies Bible class. Immediately following a morning worship service, several faithful, dedicated young ladies came to me and asked if I would try to reach their husbands. They wanted so much to have them in church with the family. The young men chose to attend services only now and then. Back in those days, young men were popular if they drove a jacked-up truck about four feet from the regular wheel base, had a gun rack behind the seat filled with rifles or shotguns, and had a plug of tobacco between their cheek and gum. The young men cared little for Bible study or worship. This was another blood clot!

One Sunday morning during one my sermon, I shared with the congregation that we had a major problem in our church and in our community. This problem was a major spiritual blood clot that needed to be addressed. On Monday evenings, our Christian witness training teams would go out into the community, sharing the gospel and inviting people to come and worship with us. As we went out, we discovered that many of these people would laugh at our church because we had leaders within our fellowship who would join them, sitting inside a bar and drinking alcoholic beverages. Those we visited would tell me that they could not come to our church because of the hypocrites that were there. I decided to share this with the church and ask for those in the congregation to have a change of heart, repent or step down from the positions they held.

Eventually, several did step down. Sometime later, during an evening service, an opportunity was given to anyone who would like to stand and give praise to God for what they had experienced lately. Several stood up and testified, and one young man stood and apologized to the church. He shared with everyone that he was one of the hypocrites. He went on to share about a certain mother who was present when he testified. She had approached him a few weeks earlier to tell him what a wonderful role model he was and how her children looked up to him. For days, the young man wrestled in his heart about being a hypocrite. That evening, while speaking to the congregation, he looked at that mother and asked her to forgive him for living a double standard. He promised everyone that he would no longer go into that liquor store because he wanted to be a faithful Christian for his Lord.

Well, he did go back into that liquor store — not to participate in drinking, but rather to take gospel tracts and revival posters and place them on the bulletin board. It is a fact that when a believer truly gets on fire for the Lord, people will come to watch him burn! God began to dissolve many blood clots that Sunday evening!

Chapter Review: Dissolving Spiritual Blood Clots (Part 1)

Psalm 46; Jeremiah 33:3

Four Killer B's
    Business meetings
    Bylaws
    Buildings
    Budgets

Lessons from churches
    My home church
    Unity Baptist Church
    Union Baptist Church

Chapter Seven

Dissolving Spiritual Blood Clots (Part 2)

And the Lord thy God will put out those nations before thee by little and little; thou mayest not consume them at once. (Deuteronomy 7:22)

The Old Testament text has meant so much to me over the years. Like so many other people, I want everything done yesterday. Our human nature desires for God to accomplish a task for us, and if it does not happen immediately, our faith decreases. We give up so easily. This is the way it is in church revitalization. We pray, asking God to turn the church around. We may even attend a two or three-day seminar, thinking that is the answer. The truth is, a seminar will only plant a few seeds. It may help, but it takes time and patience.

Consider the Israelites. They had a deed — signed, sealed, and delivered. The deed is God's Word. He had promised them the land of Canaan. He promised them that He, Himself, would put out the nations before them. The forty years of wandering in the wilderness had come to an end. The only thing between God's people and the land of promise was the narrow stream of Jordan. Soon they would be able to take possession of what God had prepared for them — in the name, and for the glory of, what God had already given them. God had promised that He would be with them and He would work for them.

Now take notice that God did not promise He would complete this with a single stroke, but He would do it slowly, "little by little." His people were to "rest in the Lord and wait patiently for Him." He said that this would be done slowly. It is imperative that a church understand this truth. Why? Why did He not do this all at once? He could have just spoken the word, and it could have all been completed at once. In 1 Corinthians 10:6, we are told that "these things were our example." As New Testament Christians, we can learn from the Old Testament.

In church revitalization, we learn that God often works with what seems to us an unusual slowness. Through the process of church revitalization, we find our Lord gradually grinding the power of evil and those things contrary to His will into fragments. You will experience God casting out the satanic forces little by little. For a church to experience this, it will take more that human skill, a degree on a wall, a three-day seminar or worldly wisdom. The inhabitants before us are evil passions, evil thoughts, worldly desires, and old habits of the past. These have to be cast out by replacing them with thoughts, desires and habits that are pure and holy, God-pleasing and God-like. How is this done? It is done by little and little!

We must understand that we are going against the tide, against flesh and blood, against all types of opposing forces. This battle is not ours, but God's. He sees the discipline that is good for us. He knows that all we will go through will prepare us for a higher service and for a holy joy that will come only through Him! God will grant your life and your church a gradual deliverance, little by little. Remember that a final success is promised. Yes, there will be a continuous warfare.

I am convinced that God does not want us to live in the valley of defeat and depression, but on the mountain top of victory! Yes, we will have our valleys in life, but He has promised many blessings that we haven't realized. We read in the book of Joshua about God giving Mt. Hebron to Caleb. It was his, but he had to believe God, go in and take what was already given. As Christians, we have God's promise: "Seek ye first the kingdom of God and His righteousness and all these things shall be added unto you" (Matthew 6:33).

In church revitalization, we have a challenge, as did Caleb and the others who spied out the promised land. In Numbers 13:23, they saw the grapes, figs, pomegranates and clusters so big it took two men to carry them on a pole. Within the church, we see before us the possibilities, and we know the promises God has made to us. As believers in Christ, we should be motivated and excited about experiencing church revitalization!

The opportunities are before us, but a problem we face is Satan hindering us. So many church members are like the spies who returned from searching out the land who fear and lack a faith to go forward. The spies saw Hebron walled and full of giants.

My friend, the devil will not give up without a fight. In Numbers 13:22, we find the word "nevertheless"; that is, when they saw this challenge of Hebron being full of giants and the great wall before them, they began to doubt and fear. Some of you have strongholds that you see, and these strongholds hinder you from witnessing a revitalization within your church. Satan does not want you to give up your strongholds. However, if we will keep our eyes on the Lord, trust in His Word and keep pressing on by faith, God will grant us victory over our enemies; that is, over our sins (spiritual blood clots). But it will be gradual, little by little.

We read in Joshua 14:1-10 that Caleb was eighty-five years old. The city was walled, giants were there and the fight was uphill. Because God had promised, "It is yours," Caleb said, "Now therefore give me this mountain … I shall be able to drive them out as the Lord said." Hebron became Caleb's inheritance because he wholly followed the Lord God of Israel (verse 14).

Yes, there is a continuous warfare. One day we will face temptation. The next day we will be encouraged. Another day we will feel defeated by it and then we will be humbled. At times we will lose ground, be humiliated and turn to prayer. As long as we continue by faith, little by little, trusting in Christ and His Word, we will be making progress! Those things that seemed impossible will become a reality. Foes who stand in the way and hinder us will give way little by little. There is a lesson to be learned. When God said, "Thou mayest not destroy them at once, lest the beasts of the field increase upon thee," we learn the lesson of humility and experience the grace of a gradual attainment. Realize that this comes through difficulty, sorrow, conflict and, at times, through defeat. God will use these things to take away our pride, manage our ambitions, and take away our vanities, selfishness and lust. Eventually we see the end-result of victory. How will this be done? It will be done by little and little.

Allow me to encourage and challenge you to beware of the "grasshopper" complex. When the other spies saw the giants, they began to see themselves as grasshoppers in their sight. When Caleb saw the giants, he saw them (the giants) as grasshoppers in God's sight! Caleb's companions who said "count me out" looked at the giants; however, Caleb looked to God and saw how much smaller the giants were than God. Caleb's companions never gained any territory and therefore wandered and died in the wilderness, just like many of our churches today. Many Christians and churches know nothing about victory because they simply want to wander and, as a result, will die in the wilderness of doom and gloom.

Caleb had courage, and you can, too! When he heard the promises of God, the giants didn't matter. God said it, and that settled it. Caleb realized God's deed was signed, sealed and delivered! In Joshua 15:14, we are told: "And Caleb drove thence the three sons of Anak, She-shai and Ahiman and Talmai, the children of Anak." God gave him three giants, and Caleb had the victory. Now may we who believe in God's Word say as the Apostle Paul: "I can do all things through Christ which strengthens me" (Philippians 4:13).

Church revitalization can be a reality if we stand upon God's Word! There is one church where I served as pastor that taught me these truths. It was at Temple Baptist Church in Simpsonville, South Carolina. This was a church full of spiritual blood clots! I was fully aware of the blood clots before I accepted the call to serve as pastor. To those who want to truly experience revitalization in your church, take heed and glean from what you are about to read!

Before accepting this call, I was very comfortable in my pastorate in Iva, South Carolina. I had attended a Bailey Smith Crusade near Atlanta, where Sam Cathey was preaching. When he stood up to preach, he spoke on "How to Experience the Power of God" in our lives. This was what I wanted to hear! Oh, how I wanted this experience! He preached from 1 Kings 18, where Elijah put the prophets of Baal to shame when he called upon His God, and "the fire of the Lord fell and consumed the burnt sacrifice, and the wood, and the stones, and the dust and licked up the water in the trench" (verse 38). When the fire of God fell and all the people saw it, they fell on their faces, and they said, "The Lord, He is God; the Lord, He is God" (verse 39).

Sam Cathey shared with us five things we must do that Elijah did to experience that power in our lives. These five things were: We must rebuild the altar, we must give an offering (a sacrifice), your most prized possession must go, you must create a situation that requires divine intervention, and we must pray the right prayer. It would take pages to share this entire message, so I want to elaborate on one part of this message in order for you to understand my accepting the call to Temple Baptist Church.

While listening to this sermon, I understood clearly about my rebuilding the altar and making this a top priority, of spending time alone with God. I also understood the second part of the message about the offering and presenting myself a living sacrifice, holy and acceptable unto God. When he shared that our most prized possession had to go (the most prized possession in Elijah's experience was water, because of the severe drought in that day), I knew what my most prized possession was: my dad's railroad watch, which was the only possession I received when he passed away. As soon as I heard that point in the message, I felt a cold chill go down my spine, as if it were a block of ice. Within my heart I knew what I was supposed to do. I gave this watch to my church in Iva, to be sold to the highest bidder; whatever amount was received, it was to go for evangelism to reach the unsaved.

When Sam Cathey shared the fourth point, I did not know how to apply it to my life. What was this point that he shared? Through this scripture, the lesson was that we are to create a situation that required divine intervention. It took some time for me to figure this one out, and I did when I accepted the call to Simpsonville. The fifth and final point I understood. My prayer was to be for God to receive all glory in order for the people to know that I am God's servant, that I have obeyed His Word and that God would turn their hearts back again.

For weeks and weeks, I prayed, asking God to reveal to me how I was to create a situation that would require divine intervention. The day finally came when it was revealed so clearly. It began to be clear when I invited Bobbi Horton, a member of Temple Baptist Church, to come and share her personal testimony on Ladies Day in our church. When she stood up to speak, she began by saying how much she had enjoyed our worship service and then stated that her church had been without a pastor for nearly two years. The following week, I received a phone call from the search committee of Temple Baptist Church. They asked to meet with me.

Now here is where the situation that requires divine intervention began. I was introduced to a church by this committee that was full of blood clots. They held nothing back. They told me their church was divided and that the committee could not agree on who should be called. I was told that their business meetings were "like Vietnam." They were two churches in one. One part of the church used Southern Baptist literature and the other part used independent literature. They had a nominating committee within the church, but the other part chose their own leaders and had a separate checking account. There was no parsonage, as they had recently sold the one they had. Here was a church that needed divine intervention. I agreed to pray over this call.

Soon after our meeting, I received an unsigned letter with no return address. The letter was printed in bold, blue ink, addressed to Rev. Danny Burnley. The writer explained to me about all the hypocrites in the church, listed their names and warned me to stay away from that church. Immediately, I knew this church was where I needed to go. The Bible tells us that Satan is an accuser of the brethren, and here was the need for divine intervention. When I accepted the call, I had only two weeks to get my children enrolled in school there. I submitted my resignation with a two-week notice, only to discover that my church in Iva had a pastor appreciation day planned! My church wanted to go ahead with this special day. This was no doubt a confirmation of my leaving because, on that Sunday, the church presented me with a check for nearly $2,000, the result of our youth selling tapes of one of my messages entitled, "Daddy's Railroad Watch." The highest bidder bought the watch with the understanding that they would give the watch back to me! On that Sunday, I received my dad's railroad watch and a financial gift. God blessed and confirmed my calling.

At a reception as the new pastor of Temple Baptist Church, a certain lady approached me and asked if I had prayed about coming to Temple. I told her that I certainly had prayed. She responded by saying, "I hope you did!" Another lady came to me, looked straight into my eyes and said, "I give you six months here." Even my secretary of this church came and informed me that she was giving me two weeks' notice because her husband was being transferred with his job to another state. Well, here I was, with no other staff, and a church full of blood clots!

When I attended my first deacon's meeting, everything went well until the very end, when a deacon shared with everyone that he was receiving a number of phone calls from angry church members over the changes that were about to take place within our church. I responded by asking all deacons to tell everyone that there would be no changes made in the first year. I asked them to encourage everyone to simply bring their Bibles to church and be ready to hear God's Word.

From that moment on, the church was called on to pray earnestly and to feed upon the Word of God. What an interesting year it was! Blood clots, blood clots ... they were everywhere! One Sunday morning after Sunday school, as I was leaving my study to enter our worship service, I smelled smoke. It was coming from the ladies' restroom. I asked a lady if she would check out the room and see if there was a fire. She explained to me there was no fire, it was just some ladies smoking. Can you believe it? Men and women would go to the restrooms each Sunday before worship and light up their cigarettes! The next week, we had "No Smoking" signs in all restrooms and fellowship hall.

Revitalization is what this church needed, and it was beyond me. Here was the situation that required divine intervention. Think about it for a moment. Here is a divided church — two churches in one — an old educational building that had not been repaired or remodeled since the late 1940s, a building that was landlocked with no way to expand, two pastors before me who had departed under terrible situations, and no staff. They were an angry congregation, digging in their heels, afraid to change. On top of all this, a certain Sunday school class had its own bank account, used other literature, and just did their own thing. They had a special day one Sunday morning by calling some seventy-five people together — men, women, boys and girls — to change the name of their class to the "Open Door Sunday School Class," open to all ages!

I could go on and on, telling of many more blood clots, but it would take an entire book to do so. Here was a church with 160 people in Sunday school, with thirty of those being counted from the nursing home ministry each Sunday. Doesn't this sound exciting? It was to me, because I knew this was where God wanted me to be.

How were these spiritual blood clots dissolved? It began by my calling on the church to turn back to God's Word. The Bible had all the answers. The church began to pray and, "little by little," God began to move.

Over time, hearts began to change. That nucleus of people within the church who wanted God to manifest Himself began to grow spiritually and numerically. The Bible says: "He that walketh with the wise shall be wise; but a companion of fools shall be destroyed" (Proverbs 13:20). The wisest man I knew concerning church growth was Aubert Rose. He had already been with me in church growth crusades. Aubert served with Dr. Charles Stanley at First Baptist Church in Atlanta when Dr. Stanley first began there. Aubert Rose has been a precious gift for my entire ministry. I learned so much from him.

I called Aubert and asked him to come and lead us in a church growth crusade. We had services on Wednesday, Thursday and Friday, had a Saturday morning visitation and a high attendance day on Sunday morning. When Aubert stood to preach, he did something I had never experienced before. He asked how many in our congregation had been members there for at least ten years or more. Many raised their hands. He then told those who had raised their hands to come forward when he gave the invitation, and he also told them to repent! He began naming the blood clots (sins) in the church and proceeded to tell them that they had allowed their church to get in a terrible situation. He addressed the beautiful worship center and the ugly educational space. He called it a shame and said they needed to repent! I thought surely many would be angry over this and I would hear about it! However, I never heard a word. As a matter of fact, after the crusade, our entire ceiling in our kitchen and fellowship hall fell in! To God be the glory! God had begun to work!

Aubert left me a list of recommendations, and he went over these with me. He shared with me from Amos 3:3: "Can two walk together except they be agreed?" He went on by telling me that the pastor and deacons needed to pray and make recommendations to the church to unify the church. He made it clear that we would lose some members, but this had to be done. After his departure, I called our deacons and dream team together. We prayed and discussed the needs.

These were some of the recommendations we presented to the church. With the deacons and planning team standing behind me, we explained Amos 3:3 and that we as leaders were in one accord with this presentation. We encouraged the church to walk together with us. We recommended that all Sunday school classes be willing to change and work together; that all classes change their literature to the Uniform Series of our convention; that we approve a master plan for renovation of our educational facilities; that we approve Sunday school restructuring of all classes into a graded system; that we do away with our old auditorium by changing it into a two-story education space for preschool, children and youth; and for us to do this together. We had already done away with our monthly business meetings. We informed them that if anyone had questions they could meet with our leaders during the next two weeks. We would then simply ask for their approval. To our surprise, there was nearly a 98 percent vote of approval! A miracle had taken place!

Now allow me to fast forward. God blessed by allowing me to serve as their pastor for some thirteen years. A long-range master plan was later approved for a new family life center, a new worship center and new educational facilities. The family life center has been completed under the direction of the last two pastors. The church's next goal is to build a new worship center, God willing. They have also purchased every house and all property on the entire block!

When I left Temple Baptist Church, we were averaging 288 in Sunday school and had a high attendance day of over 400. Dr. Brad Whitt became their pastor, serving twelve years, and Brett Atkins has been serving nearly four years. These two men of God have been a blessing to this wonderful church, and the people so love their pastors!

If this church can experience revitalization, your church can, also, if only you will follow the steps in this book which are based on the Word of God. Take courage!

Chapter Review: Dissolving Spiritual Blood Clots (Part 2)

Deuteronomy 7:22

God's Promise to the Israelites

God's Promise to the Church
    1 Corinthians 10:6; Matthew 6:33

Caleb's Challenge
    The Possibilities
    Numbers 13:23
    The Problem
    Numbers 13:22; Joshua 14:10-13, 14

Caleb's Companions

Caleb's Courage
    Joshua 15:14; Philippians 4:13

Caleb's Conquest
    1 Kings 18:38-39; Amos 3:3

Chapter Eight

DEALING WITH SPIRITUAL STROKES

But God forbid that I should glory, save in the cross of our Lord Jesus Christ by whom the world is crucified unto me, and I unto the world. (Galatians 6:14)

One thing needs to be very clear about this book: It is not meant to be all about me; rather, it is all about Jesus Christ and His Word. My desire and goal is simply to share with you and your church and to encourage the saints. The churches that you are reading about are real. They are not megachurches, but they are now churches with a fresh renewal and a new excitement. As for me, I am what I am by the grace of God if I am anything (Galatians 5:10). I pray that some dear saint of God, some dear pastor, or some dear church, will be blessed from the writing of this book. My greatest joy has come from working with churches that have lost their joy, and then witnessing dear believers being revitalized through the Word of God.

Revitalization begins by admitting there are spiritual blood clots within the church. One of those churches is Laurel Baptist Church in Greenville, South Carolina. This church was so very close to closing her doors and selling the property to a business next door.

It was March of 2011 when Delano McMinn, a retired director of missions in Anderson, South Carolina, called me. He began to tell me about Laurel Baptist Church and its sad condition. The search committee had met with Delano on several occasions and asked him to serve as their interim pastor. He explained to them that they were about to close the doors of the church and that their need was not for an interim pastor but a full-time pastor. This was a most serious time for their church.

Before I was contacted by Delano, Laurel had come to the realization of just how desperate they were. Thanks be to God, the members had humbled themselves, begun to pray and seek the face of God, turning to Him for help and deliverance. By God's grace, He led Delano McMinn to them. The church was now ready to listen to this man of God as he shared biblical direction for them to follow.

When Delano called me in March, he asked if I would sit down with the search committee and share with them the steps I followed in helping churches refocus and experience renewal. I agreed to help where I could. At the first meeting with the search committee, they explained very clearly their situation. The Sunday school and worship services averaged around thirty in attendance. There was about $1,100 coming in weekly through their offerings, and they were collecting an annual missions offering of approximately $1,800. This included the Annie Armstrong, Janie Chapman and Lottie Moon offerings, along with other missions offerings that were given during that year.

The committee was made up of only four precious senior saints. They wanted so much to see their church turn around. We continued meeting through the month of October. It was not my desire or intention to become the pastor of such a difficult situation. It was my desire to retire from the pastorate at that time. God, however, had different plans. Eventually, they presented me with a copy of their nominating committee report, listing the officers and teachers. The list looked so pitiful. There was only one children's class, where only two or three children attended. There was no youth class, nor were there any young adults attending. This was one of the saddest church situations I had ever seen. There were plenty of facilities available, including a large worship center, a three-story educational facility, a family life center, a chapel-fellowship hall, a large basement with classrooms, numerous other classrooms and a number of office spaces. The only staff member using an office space was a financial secretary. There were two excellent musicians helping the church, but the facilities were in so much need.

The sound system being used was installed back in the 1970s. The third floor of the educational facility was not being used and had not been renovated since it was built. The basement had not been used in many years. Several heating and air-conditioning units needed to be replaced, the children's wing needed to be renovated, much painting needed to be done, the roofing for both the children's facility and the family life center needed to be replaced, and office spaces were empty of staff personnel. This church was at an all-time low.

At one of our meetings, the search committee handed me a copy of the church's bylaws. After studying these, I told the committee that their bylaws were a large blood clot. There was no way to go by them and to be able to pastor biblically at the same time. Delano McMinn called me soon afterward, asking what changes I would suggest. My response was for the church to do away with the bylaws and start all over afresh. Their bylaws kept the pastor and church in bondage. To my surprise, the search committee, with the advice of Delano McMinn, mailed a letter to the membership, recommending that Laurel Baptist Church do away with the bylaws. A miracle took place — the church voted 100 percent to do away with the bylaws!

Imagine what I was thinking! When I went to bed that night, there was no way I could sleep! Psalm 6:6 describes my experience: "All the night make I my bed to swim." Early the next morning, I called Delano to ask the leadership if they would contact Paul Fleming, who was on staff at Forestville Baptist Church in Greenville, and have him come and explain the ACTS ministry. Laurel Baptist Church could adopt similar bylaws and have a fresh course of direction. Paul Fleming came on a Friday and addressed the church on Sunday. On Monday, the search committee sent out a letter to all members of the church with a recommendation that the church adopt the ACTS ministry plan and attend the ACTS ministry training. Laurel Baptist Church again voted 100 percent to approve this direction.

Here I was, with all green lights given to me by God, Himself, to take on this great challenge in helping another church through revitalization! At our last meeting, Linda Miller of the committee asked, "What will it take for you to come and be our pastor?" Bill Heath, the eldest on the committee said, "Pastor, we need your help." After months of prayer, meetings and adjustments, God, no doubt, called me to serve as their new pastor. It had been my plan to retire, and today I praise Him for this honor and privilege to serve with these dear people. Laurel Baptist Church learned that revitalization begins by admitting there are spiritual blood clots. Revitalization continues by dealing with the spiritual stroke!

If there is a passage of scripture that this church reminds me of, it would be John 11. It is the story of Lazarus when he was sick and near death, and his sisters sent word to Jesus about his condition. These sisters describe the small remnant from Laurel Baptist Church. There were those within its membership who asked earnestly for the Lord's divine intervention. Jesus not only loved Martha, her sister and Lazarus, He also loved Laurel Baptist Church. To those who sincerely desire church revitalization, it must first be understood that it begins by the humbling of ourselves and calling upon our Lord Jesus for help.

When Jesus arrived on the scene, Martha said unto Jesus, "Lord, if Thou hadst been here, my brother had not died." Now what about us, dear church? Where is Jesus? Do we not remember His promise from Matthew 28:20 when He said, "And lo, I am with you always, even unto the end of the world. Amen."? Hebrews 13:5 also promises that He "will never leave thee, nor forsake thee." Chapter 13:6 tells us: "The Lord is my Helper and I will not fear," and, in verse 8: "Jesus Christ the same, yesterday, and today, and forever." Our Lord is with us today. Let us humble ourselves and begin crying out to our Lord. He is ready, willing and able to help us. He loves the church, and that is what makes it so exciting — to watch God begin to move in our midst.

Laurel Baptist Church was considered dead by so many. Jesus said, "I am the resurrection and the life; he that believeth in me though he were dead, yet shall he live; And whosoever liveth and believeth in me shall never die, believest thou this?" (verses 25-26).

What about you, pastor? What about you, deacon? What about you, Sunday school teacher, church member? Do you believe God's Word? I submit unto you: A very small nucleus from Laurel Baptist Church believed! In John 11:39, Jesus said, "Take away the stone." I ask you, my friend, which stone stands between you and your believing God to do a miracle (or miracles) within your church? Jesus told Martha, in verse 40, "If thou wouldst believe, thou wouldst see the glory of God." Praise God — they then took away the stone from where the dead was laid!

The members of Laurel Baptist Church began moving the stone before them out of the way. We all began dealing with spiritual blood clots — not only by praying, but also by believing God's Word. Faith produced action, and God began to move. Allow me to share what God began to do.

After I became a pastor, a young man came to my study. He was Mike Conklin, a bi-vocational minister of students from another church. After introducing himself, he told me that a pastor had informed him of our need for a youth minister. I explained to him that we had many needs, but little income; we would have to wait a while before bringing on another staff member. We shared the Word of God and prayed together.

A few weeks later, Mike returned and said that he believed God was in my calling to pastor Laurel Church and that he would like to come and help me. He had a good job and was willing to come on a volunteer basis. He was invited to attend a meeting with our deacons and pastor to share his personal testimony. Afterwards, we asked him to share his testimony with our church with the understanding that we would recommend our call to him in serving as our minister of students.

When we shared with the congregation about his coming on a volunteer basis, unknown to us, there was a couple in their early 80s visiting with us on that Sunday. After the service, the elderly couple asked if they might meet with me the next morning. We met together, and the couple wanted to commit to giving $150 weekly for one year in order to help the minister of students with his gas and meals. They also committed to giving $3,000 toward our youth ministry, $3,000 toward our children's ministry, $2,300 for our evangelism ministry, and $1,500 for the improvements for our children's wing and also other improvements for our church! Glory to God!

Following this, during a midweek prayer service, Carlos and Rita Galarza, a Hispanic couple, came in. After the prayer service, they shared with me their heartfelt desire to begin a new Hispanic ministry and wanted to know if our church could use them. I took them downstairs to our basement area and showed them the possibilities. They were excited! Carlos and Rita both had jobs and were willing to serve bi-vocationally. Today, they are still with us. We have a wonderful Hispanic group and also have begun a new church ministry in Mexico. How was all this happening? Our answer: It is a God thing.

Soon after this, as our offerings increased, we called Tony Serrao as our minister of worship. Though we are by no means a large church (yet), we loved our choir, musicians and staff — and we were excited!

Dr. Danny Settle appeared on the scene. He was a close friend and pastor who had decided to leave a ministry he was leading and began attending our church. He asked if he might unite with us, with the understanding he would probably be moving to another ministry soon. I invited him to come aboard and help us. After a few months, he, too, approached me about his willingness to come and help me on a volunteer basis. He believed God would take care of his needs. He was so correct! He now serves as our minister of education and has been a blessing to us.

After about three years, our minister of students began a new ministry in helping the hungry and the homeless. God continues to bless him. Immediately, God blessed us with another young family, Asbury and Ashley Lawton, to serve in his place! Can you not see how God has worked? We have completed many of our renovations, we have a wonderful staff, and our church is out of debt. Praise the Lord!

As we turn our attention back to the book of John, we read, "Lazarus, come forth" (verse 43). Here is where excitement begins to build! We are told in verse 44, "He that was dead came forth. When he came forth (now, don't miss this) he was "bound hand and foot with grave clothes; and his face was bound about with a napkin." What can we learn from this in regards to church revitalization? We can learn that God has more wonderful things ahead for us that we cannot imagine! Ephesians 3:20-21 motivates us: "Now unto him that is able to do exceeding abundantly above all that we ask or think according to the power in us, unto him be glory in the church, by Christ Jesus throughout all ages, world without end. Amen."

Note the words: "according to the power in us." In order for us to come forth and experience the power of God, we, too, must die to ourselves, to our whims, to our selfish desires, and allow God to take control. The Bible says: "Ye receive not because you ask not" (James 4:2). The Bible also says: "Ye receive not because ye ask amiss that ye may consume it upon your own lusts" (James 4:3). Church revitalization is for God's glory. It is all about Him and His Son, and allowing His Holy Spirit to take control. To Him be all glory and praise!

John Mullis entered my study one day and placed a number of books and old records on my desk. He shared with me his lack of desire to change our bylaws and to enter the ACTS ministry, among other things. He also shared about the night before, when God spoke to his heart, reminding him of his prayers when John asked God to turn the church around. He went on to say that God told him to get out of the way; the church has turned around! John then said he wanted to help me — and he has! God is using him as a prayer partner of mine and a Sunday school teacher, and he serves on our hospitalization and building ministries.

At Easter, we celebrate the resurrection of our Lord Jesus Christ. We concentrate on His resurrection, but we must remember that before there could be a resurrection, Jesus had to be willing to die! He did die, and He rose from the grave. There are those who are leaders and members of our churches who talk revitalization but are not willing to allow Christ to have control. Jesus Christ and His Word must be in control. We must be willing to die to ourselves. Picture Lazarus after coming forth from the grave, "bound hand and foot with grave clothes." Even his face was bound with a napkin! Lazarus came forth, but he could not see nor move in any direction until he was loosed from his grave clothes. So it is with the church!

Jesus then spoke to those around Lazarus, saying, "Loose him, and let him go" (John 11:44). What does this have to do with Laurel Baptist Church? It had been over four years since I became their pastor. As those who witnessed Lazarus coming from the grave, so have many of us witnessed Laurel Baptist Church coming from the grave, as well. This was wonderful, yet God had revealed to this pastor two major spiritual blood clots in the church. They had been there for a number of years, and they were the main cause of decline and spiritual stroke over the years. The blood clots were very clear!

What were these two blood clots that remained? First, there were so many policies that hindered the reaching of souls for Christ. Like forensic files, the church's DNA could be traced back for many years. What is this DNA? It is what makes you uniquely you and why you resemble your parents. It is a genetic formation whereby forensics can trace your blood line back for years! What does this have to do with the church? What does this have to do with church revitalization? Just look back at this church in the 1970s, when it was a soul winning, Bible-believing church with a desire for growth. It was filled to capacity There were times back in those days when the church had to put chairs down the aisles because so many were attending! What happened? The answer is simple: Blood clots began to form, which later caused this church to have a spiritual stroke. Where were the blood clots? One was in the "policies" of the church.

Before I became the pastor, the church came to realize that the bylaws were so filled with rules and regulations that the church could hardly breathe. There were so many dos and don'ts and restrictions and requirements demanded of its membership. After eliminating the bylaws and beginning anew, the church began to flourish again. There have been times when, as pastor, I could not sense the freedom we needed to accomplish what I believed God wanted us to do — to grow the church in the power and demonstration of the Holy Spirit. There seemed to be a snag somewhere.

One day our deacon chairman asked our office manager to pull up our policies to review. He brought them by my study and asked me to look over them. To our surprise, there were policies on file which the deacons nor pastor were aware of. All a person had to do was write up a policy and drop it in the policy file. When this was brought to our attention, we shared this with the church, set up a policy review team and made the necessary corrections, with the understanding of the church that any policy regarding the church must receive a stamp of approval noting that the policy had been reviewed and approved by the leadership of the church. Policies were worse than the bylaws. It was a DNA problem that had existed for years.

Another blood clot that hindered spiritual and numerical growth was the buildings themselves. The buildings were dedicated to the Lord when they were built, but over the years the buildings hindered the growth of the church. How could this be? Because of a DNA problem that began after the 1970s, the church began declining. The buildings, which began as a good thing, turned out to be a bad thing. Instead of wanting to see the church filled to capacity, policies and procedures would not allow this to become a reality.

Right after I became pastor, I challenged the men to set a goal of having at least forty men to give $100 each to help bring in a very wonderful, well-known gospel singing group. These funds would take care of all expenses, travel, lodging and honorarium. By doing this, we would have another goal to fill the church to capacity, take up a special love offering and give it all to the Gideons ministry to purchase Bibles. What an exciting time! Tickets were made up, promotions were made everywhere possible, and there was excitement in the air. We had such a wonderful response, to the point of having an overflow crowd in another part of the church.

About two weeks before the concert, someone called the fire department and requested that they come and tell us how many people could sit in our facilities. Can you believe it? How ridiculous! scripture tells us the Master said to His servants, "Go into the highways and hedges and compel them to come in that My house may be filled." This was not a suggestion; it was an instruction given by the Master Himself! Because of ridiculous policies, procedures and ignorance of the Word of God, hundreds were turned away.

Satan did not, and does not, want a lost and dying world to enter the house of God to hear the message of salvation. In all my years of living, I had never experienced such a satanic attack. Whenever buildings take precedence over baptisms, and policies are more important than people, buildings and policies become gods, the Holy Spirit is quenched and you have a major blood clot that will eventually produce a stroke.

Dr. Michael Duduit, dean of the College of Christian Studies at Anderson University, spoke to sixty or seventy men at a men's breakfast. He spoke on the subject, "When Good Things Go Bad." He used as his text Numbers 21, where the people spoke against God and against Moses. The Lord sent fiery serpents among the people, biting them; as a result, many people died. When the people confessed to Moses that they had sinned,

Moses prayed for the people. The Lord told Moses to make a fiery serpent and set it on a pole so that everyone who is bitten, when he looked upon it, would live. This was good!

Moving on to 2 Kings 18, however, Hezekiah began to reign, and we are told: "And he did that which was right in the sight of the Lord, according to all that David his father did. He removed the high places, and broke in pieces the images, and cut down the groves and broke in pieces the brazen serpent that Moses had made: for unto those days the children of Israel did burn incense to it; and he called it Nehushtan" (verses 3-4). Hezekiah destroyed the brazen serpent because what was meant for good was being worshipped, and it turned out to be bad! So it is with church buildings if we are not careful.

Dr. Duduit went on to tell us about an experience he had years earlier when he began his ministry as a minister of youth. He told of a special night at the church where he was serving. Many young people turned out, revival broke out and souls were being saved. It was one of the most thrilling times in his ministry. That was good — until the next day, when he was called in and had to face the leadership of the church, where he received a stern scolding from a women's Sunday school class because the youth had moved their chairs! And we wonder today where our youth and young adults are?

I suggested to our church that, even though our family life center was on our dream team's list to be renovated, let us drop the renovation part. It would keep us from spending thousands of dollars on such a project. It would be unnecessary to paint the walls, refinish the floors, replace the lights, install new insulation and modernize our backboards. If all this was done, a basketball might not be allowed on the floor of our gym. Lights would be hit, balls would bounce off the newly painted walls, and the backboards would be damaged. As a result, the family life center would be placed on "lockdown"!

If a church is ever going to be revitalized, we must confess our sins (our blood clots) and determine if we are serious about the Word of God and reaching souls — or if we more concerned about policies than people and buildings over baptisms.

Remember, revitalization becomes a reality when we obey the Great Physician. Jesus promised us that He is near, and He will never leave us or forsake us. Jesus hears us when we call to Him; He says, "Call unto Me and I will answer thee and shew thee great and mighty things which thou knowest not" (Jeremiah 33:3). He cares for us! He promised: "My God shall supply all of [our] needs according to His riches in glory in Christ Jesus: (Philippians 4:19).

Laurel Baptist Church has learned that Jesus will respond to our prayers when we confess our sins — our spiritual blood clots — as we turn to Him and put away those things that have become gods to us (things that once were good but have become evil). When the spiritual blood clots are dealt with, Jesus informs us, through His Word and through our prayers, what we should do. He is calling us today to focus on Him and His Word. His Word is clear to us when we draw near to Him. He is ready, willing and able to help us and guide us. Let's get serious about church revitalization. Let's go forward in Jesus' name!

Chapter Review: Dealing with Spiritual Strokes

Galatians 6:14

Revitalization begins by admitting there are spiritual blood clots

Revitalization continues by dealing with the spiritual stroke

Revitalization becomes a reality when we obey the Great Physician (John 11:1-45)

Jesus is near
Jesus hears
Jesus cares
Jesus responds
Jesus informs
Jesus calls
Jesus clarifies

Chapter Nine

Creating Balance Within the Church

Ponder the path of thy feet, and let all thy ways be established. (Proverbs 4:26)

Anyone who has served the Lord in ministry for a time will tell you that everyone has an opinion. Most everyone will tell you what to do and what you should not do. If not careful, a person on fire for God can grow spiritually cross-eyed by those who seem to know it all. So it is within the church, especially when there is the need for revitalization. Opinions, they come from everywhere, even from good church people. I have my opinion, as well, but the only source we can trust is the Word of God.

Upon entering the ministry to preach the gospel and becoming a pastor, I had both barrels loaded and the trigger cocked, ready to go — I thought! I was like a bull in a china shop. My heart's desire was to reach lost people and grow a church. When I became the pastor of Union Baptist Church, my first full-time pastorate, in January of 1983, I was ready to take off! After only five months as pastor there, God put the brakes on. He stopped me and began to teach me about balance in my personal life. Balance is the key to a successful ministry in the eyes of God. He tells us to "ponder" our path and "let all [our] ways be established."

In order to revitalize our church, we must first have our own personal lives in balance. No one was more sincere than I was about pleasing God and wanting to see the church go forward and grow. I poured my heart and soul into the ministry. As pastor, I preached on Sunday morning and evening. My message was prepared for Wednesday evening. On Monday evenings, we began Continual Witness Training to teach members how to go into homes and share the gospel. Everything had to be organized — from the CWT class to the names of those we were to visit, including their address and phone number. This took so much time!

Since there was no young adult Sunday school class, I decided to start one. In addition, I also began a discipleship training class. Added to all of this were the different ministries, including hospital and nursing home visitation, committee meetings, counseling sessions, associational meetings, etc., etc. Also, by May, which was only four months away, all of my studies for graduation had to be completed and turned in. As the old saying goes, "I was burning the midnight oil."

On a beautiful, sunny day, I was traveling down Highway 81, returning home from visiting at the hospital. It was a day I shall never forget. While riding, I noticed a telephone pole to my right. As I drew closer to it, the pole seemed to disappear. One second it was there, then it was gone. To my left, there was an automobile about to pass by me in the other lane. One moment it was there, then it disappeared. I looked down and could see my right hand, but not my left hand. Arriving home, I went to my bedroom to lie down. My vision was so blurred. My wife was leaving to go shopping, but she was concerned about me. I encouraged her to go ahead, and I would simply rest a while. After her departure, our phone began to ring. It was a call from a lady in our church whose name was Mary Beth Bruce. Suddenly, everything became confused. Why would she have three names? After hanging up the phone, I decided to look into our church file to find her name. All the letters in the alphabet ran together, and I was unable to locate the name. As I lay on the bed, the twenty-third psalm came to me so clearly. How could I quote the psalm and not be able to figure out the name or the alphabet?

I decided to call a doctor, but I was unable to read the phone numbers and names. It was so confusing and troubling. A panic attack began to set in. All I knew to do was press "0" for operator. After explaining my situation, the operator connected me with a local doctor, who asked me to come in immediately. When my two young boys arrived home from school, they were able to help me get to the doctor's office. After a thorough examination, the doctor told me that my problem was one of two things. It was either the result of being under a lot of stress, or it was a brain tumor. The doctor was a devout Christian, and he asked if I was familiar with the New Testament scripture where Jesus told his disciples, "Come ye yourselves apart into a desert place, and rest a while" (Mark 6:31). When I told him I was familiar with the scripture, he responded by telling me that was what I must do. He asked if I had a hobby. My response was, "Church." I ate, breathed and loved the church. As it says in verse 31, "there were many coming and going, and they had no leisure so much as to eat." Neither did I.

During the month of May, with a graduation date set, my family prepared to travel from South Carolina to Evansville, Indiana. It was my desire to leave early on Monday morning, travel for eleven hours, spend the night in a nice hotel, then get up the next morning and enjoy the entire day with my family. The very next morning, after a good night's sleep, I was shaving, preparing to go out for breakfast with my family. Suddenly, it happened again. Part of the mirror began to disappear. Only part of my body, the mirror and the room could be seen. It was what is called "tube vision." My wife drove the family to a restaurant for breakfast. My head felt as if it was about to split. It was as if an ice pick was going through my head. A waitress gave me two Excedrin, but there was no pain relief at all. My wife called Trinity College of the Bible and asked someone about a doctor. They made an appointment for us, and the doctor told me the same thing as did the doctor back home. What was I to do? To whom could I turn? The medicine I received that day caused me to sleep for a number of hours. It was a most difficult time in my life.

The next day, I sat with several hundred people. I was near the back of the room, discouraged about my family, frustrated over the ministry, questioning God, and asking the Lord what I should do. God had me right where He wanted me to be. My friend, God has you right where He wants YOU to be. He has your church right where He wants it to be as well.

The president of the school introduced our guest speaker. He was Dr. Harold Hunter, pastor of First Baptist Church of North Jacksonville, Florida. When Dr. Hunter arose to address the assembly, he shared with us how God had laid upon his heart to speak on the subject, "Dealing with Stress in Ministry". Thank God! Praise God! This was exactly what I needed to hear! Glory!

Dr. Hunter shared with us that our priorities should be in order so that stress in the ministry could be relieved. Here are the five priorities that have helped me over the past thirty-three years. Write these down in your Bibles. Share them with others — pastors, deacons, teachers and parents.

First, spend your first hour of every day alone with God. Dr. Hunter stated clearly for us to use that time talking to God and allowing Him to speak to us through His Holy Word. This time is not for preparing a sermon or to teach a class, but only for an intimate time with God. This is the first step in relieving stress!

Second, spend quality time with your spouse. Do not wait until July 4th or for any vacation time to spend time together. Put an appointment on your calendar every week for you and your wife alone. This time is not to be spent only at night, but a day should be set aside every week!

Third, spend quality time with your children. Do not wait for that vacation. Here is where I became convicted! I was so busy working with other people that my children were being neglected. When did I have time to spend with them or with my wife outside of church? That day, I began making changes immediately!

Fourth, cut your cholesterol. Eat healthy foods. Cut out pork and fatty foods.

Fifth, exercise. You don't have to do this every day, but at least three or four times weekly for at least fifteen to twenty minutes.

It works! Thirty-three years later, it is still working! Let us get our personal priorities in order, and then let us prioritize for church revitalization!

Since the time God revealed these five priorities for my personal life, He has also revealed six priorities for the church. The pastor, deacons, teachers and all other leaders should understand clearly these priorities in order for the church to be revitalized. When the six priorities are in place, there will definitely be a balance in the church.

Number one: prayer. From Nehemiah 1, we read of Nehemiah hearing of the city walls of Jerusalem being torn down and the gates of the city being burned. What did Nehemiah do? First and foremost, he prayed to God! Through his prayer, he confessed his sins and the sins of Israel to God. He sat down and wept, mourned for days, and fasted. To have a balance within the church, we begin with prayer, continue in prayer, and never forget God through prayer. So many of us are so busy, we do not have time to pray. Others are so educated and so smart, they begin to think they can do things themselves, but they cannot. We need God and His wisdom in every decision and in everything we do.

Begin now having a balance in your life and church. Hebrews 10 tells us that we have access to God Himself. When our Savior, the Lord Jesus Christ, died upon the cross, the veil in the temple was rent in twain, and because of this you and I can come to God. Through His crucifixion and through His death, the way to God is open for us. If you desire church revitalization, understand that we have boldness to come into God's presence! We are encouraged by God, Himself: "Let us draw near … in full assurance of faith" (verse 22). Let us not only talk about faith, but also let us act upon our faith. Begin now, praying in the name of our Lord Jesus Christ. Pray for church revitalization. Draw near to Him with a true heart in full assurance of faith!

Number two: evangelism. God loves His church and wants His church to grow. Spiritual power and the means to revitalize the church are provided when we rely upon our Lord and follow His instructions. You are now reading from a writer who has served in perhaps all areas of the church with the exception of the ladies' ministry director. Busy, busy, busy, this writer has been. However, years ago, I came to realize that busy, busy means very little if souls are not coming to Christ. I was a Christian for a number of years before I realized that evangelism is not only for the pastor. I am ashamed to admit that it was sometime after being ordained as a deacon before learning the plan of salvation. After enrolling in Bible college, I set up files dealing with doctrine. Some of these files included theology, christology, pneumatology, soteriology, eschatology, angelology, demonology, etc. Sounds good, doesn't it? Years later, I came to realize that it would have been much better if I had spent more time learning the plan of salvation and sharing the gospel. The Bible makes it clear: Jesus came "to seek and to save that which was lost." He also promised, "Come ye after Me, and I will make you fishers of men" (Mark 1:17). We were saved to reach the lost from sin! In 2 Corinthians 5, we are told that God has given to us "the ministry of reconciliation" and He has also "committed unto us the ministry of reconciliation" (verses18-19).

If a church will commit to prayer and evangelism, the people will experience the beginning of revitalization. Here lies the joy of the church! The greatest joy one will ever experience is leading a soul to Christ. If soul-winning is not the top priority of your church, you will not have the joy that Christ has to offer, and everything will become only a ritual.

Number three: discipleship. It may be that many churches no longer have discipleship training as it was some thirty years ago because the classes became so boring and churches were always trying to find something exciting to teach in order to keep such a program from discontinuing. Let's face it: There are some programs and activities that should be buried — but not discipleship. In our modern day, we do have an interest in growing churches. We want to reach more people, yet we are doing so little in making disciples. Over the years, I have attended so many discipleship training classes, and they were great classes. The number one class that could have helped me the most would have been a class on how to lead a soul to Christ.

Outreach visitation is good, but it is so much better when you know how to lead a lost soul to Christ. When a sinner comes to know Christ as his or her Lord and Savior, that person should be given the opportunity to attend a class on soul-winning. Years went by, and I never had a clue about leading someone to Christ. I have enjoyed weekly visitation programs, inviting many to Christ, but think about how many more souls would be saved today if I had known how to witness! The greatest spiritual maturity one can experience is through leading a soul to the Savior. Christians who have had this experience will tell you that it will keep you on fire for Jesus! There is no greater joy.

In order to make disciples, we must first introduce the lost to Jesus and tell them how to be saved. Some believers will tell you that soul-winning is not their gift. My friend, this is not a gift — it is a command. The Great Commission is clear: "Go ye therefore, and teach all nations, baptizing them in the name of the Father, and of the Son, and of the Holy Ghost: teaching them to observe all things whatsoever I have commanded you" (Matthew 18:19-20). If there are to be baptisms, there must be soul-winners. If there are going to be soul-winners, there must be discipleship. We must get out from behind our stained glass windows and our wall-to-wall carpeting and engage others with the gospel.

Making disciples and marking disciples in baptism will definitely help mature the saints. This is not a suggestion, but a command from our Lord! We should be serious about discipleship by taking up our cross daily and following Him.

One of the weakest spots in the church has been with teachers and deacons. We have those within our fellowship who have been saved and soon afterward are placed in classes as teachers and are ordained as deacons without having a clue about doctrine or how to find scriptures dealing with problems. In a number of churches, a new members class is required in order for anyone to unite with the church. This class helps the newborn saints and others to mature, to become like Christ, to think like Christ, and to live an uncompromised life.

Number four: ministry. If we could only learn the process of involving as many of our church members as possible in ministry, we would become a very exciting church for the glory of God. Consider this for a moment: So many church members are like me as I grew up in and around the church. For many years, I always thought that the only ones who were "called" into the ministry were pastors. How many times have you heard someone say, "He is going to be a preacher. He has been called into the ministry." Only God knows how many times I sat in a worship service thinking about someone else who has been "called" or someone who should be "called" because I saw person who seemed to be "gifted" for the ministry. For years, I never considered myself to be a "minister." I did not see myself qualified or justified to be a minister.

Now, having become a minister, I have realized how shallow we are in regards to the calling of a minister. Have you ever stopped and considered just what a minister is? In short, a minister is a believer who meets the need of another in the name of Jesus! Christian ministry is doing good things for others with the purpose of relating them to Jesus Christ. Jesus tells us, "Whosoever will be great among you, let him be your minister; and whosoever will be chief among you, let him be your servant; even the Son of Man came not to be ministered unto, but to minister and to give his life a ransom for many" (Matthew 20:26-28).

We have so many members on our church rolls who truly love our Lord and who want to serve Him in some way, but they either do not know how or they think the pastor who has been "called" is the one who is to minister. Through prayer, evangelism and discipleship, our goal is to equip the saints to do the work of the ministry. Because of the importance of ministry, Ephesians 4:11-12 is written primarily for the purpose of engaging others in ministry. When a church begins to realize the importance of discipling others in ministry, revitalization becomes a reality. Our ministry begins in church and then extends to a lost and dying world!

Number five: fellowship. Where does fellowship begin? It begins the moment we receive Jesus Christ as our Lord and Savior. By God's grace and mercy, we become children of God, and we all have the same Father. We become a part of the family of God and are brothers and sisters in Christ. Here is a great time to check our spiritual pulse. According to Acts 2:46-47, we find the early church "continuing daily with one accord in the temple and breaking bread from house to house ... with gladness and singleness of heart, praising God and having favor with all the people." Here is one of the ways we can be sure of our salvation: Not only do we profess Christ as Lord, we also have a deep desire to fellowship with other believers! We love the church because we are His body! We love the Lord's day, when the church comes together in Bible fellowship and worship!

If you profess to be a Christian and have no desire to be with other believers according to Acts 2, how can you love Christ, who is the head of the church, without loving the church which is His body? You cannot do so! Either you are actually lost without Christ, or you are in a terribly backslidden condition. You are missing out on the joy of being in Christ! The early church experienced a bond in Christ by being together in one accord. So it is today, as we come together on Sundays and Wednesdays to fellowship with the saints.

As we think about church revitalization, we must admit that in any church where fellowship is broken, the spiritual equilibrium is out of balance and out of fellowship with our Lord. Balance consists of prayer, evangelism, discipleship, ministry, fellowship and worship. Fellowship is of utmost importance. If a church is involved in a great outreach/evangelism ministry, and those who become saved or prospects decide to visit your church and they do not see a warm, loving fellowship, they will not return. It is time for us to learn why so many do not attend our churches. Do we not understand that the Holy Spirit is quenched when there is coldness, tensions, bickering, murmuring and fighting within such a church? As people attend our churches, they need to experience love, joy, peace and encouragement. They need to witness the body of Christ bringing honor to Him through these six functions. Dr. Harold Hunter once said, "The greatest visitation program takes place on Sunday mornings when guests attend our worship services. If they don't experience the presence of the Lord among the people, they will not return."

Number six: worship. While I was attending Emmanuel College, a Pentecostal school, Dr. Melton was the president and, knowing I was a Baptist, made a truthful statement about our denomination. Think about it, because it makes so much sense. He said, "If Baptists could learn how to worship, and Pentecostals could learn how to repent, we would have a great combination." How true! Much can be said and written about worship. What we call worship today troubles me. It is so sad to see churches dividing over what some call worship. Worship does not divide the body of Christ. Worship glorifies Christ and edifies the church. It appears to me that our attention is on the music rather than the Master of the music. It is not my desire to concentrate on music styles but instead to encourage the church to emphasize worship. We know our church is in balance through worship when our goal is to have an encounter with God. A wonderful place to discover this reality is not in a song book, but in the Bible. From Isaiah 6, we find Isaiah having such an encounter. He entered the temple, and the worship service began with an awareness of who God is. In verses 1-3, He saw the Lord! He was in awe of the sovereignty and character of God. He says, "I saw also the Lord" and gives the description of God: "Holy, holy, holy is the Lord of Hosts; the whole earth is full of His glory."

My friend, the goal of a worship service begins with the awareness of who God is! When people enter our services, we want them to have an experience with God. A plaque on the very top of the pulpit where I pastor has the words engraved: "We Would See Jesus." Long ago, a pastor had this placed upon the pulpit to remind every preacher, every singer, every testimony and everyone else to remember the purpose of our being there: to lift up to Jesus!

Worship beings with the awareness of who God is, and worship involves confessing and admitting our own sinfulness. In verse 5, Isaiah says, "Woe is me! For I am undone; because I am a man of unclean lips." He was simply saying, "I am a sinner!" The closer you are to God, the more you realize you are a sinner. The further away from God, the less aware you are of your sin. When Isaiah saw the Lord as holy, holy, holy and himself a sinner, God touched him when he confessed and took away his sin. Our altars are so empty today because of a lack of awareness of the presence of God. When was the last worship service in which you had an encounter with God?

Notice in the text, Isaiah first had an awareness of God, confessed and admitted his sinfulness to God and this then led him to see the need for brokenness on the part of others. In verse 5, Isaiah continues: "I dwell in the midst of a people of unclean lips; for mine eyes have seen the King, the Lord of Hosts." We do not have to go beyond our worship center to see the results of sin and hurting people. We see the results of divorce, sodomy, abortion, drugs, alcohol, pornography, sickness and death. The psalmist, David, while hiding from King Saul in a cave, said, "I looked on my right hand and beheld, but there was no man that would know me; refuge failed me; no man cared for my soul" (Psalm 142:4).

When we have an encounter with God as Isaiah did, we see ourselves, we see others, and we realize the answer to all of our needs. It is God, Himself, and we understand He cares for us. An encounter with God then draws us to the call of Christian service. Isaiah then said, "Also I heard a voice of the Lord saying, whom shall I send, and who will go for us? Then said I, here am I; send me." When Isaiah heard God's voice, he was not drafted, coerced or forced, but rather he wanted to be involved. He totally surrendered to the call of God. Now this is true worship!

Mission opportunities are everywhere. Church revitalization is possible. Be encouraged. Begin revitalizing your church by implementing these six goals and creating a balance within your church.

Chapter Review: Creating Balance Within the Church

Proverbs 4:26

Five Personal Priorities
     Time with God alone
     Time with your spouse
     Time with your children
     Eat healthy foods
     Exercise

Six Priorities in the Church
     Prayer
     Evangelism
     Discipleship
     Ministry
     Fellowship
     Worship

Chapter Ten

BUILDING UP BIBLE FELLOWSHIP

My people are destroyed for lack of knowledge. (Hosea 4:6)

As we look at America today, we must admit that we are in a deplorable state of spiritual debility. Most of our churches are in a decline, and it seems we are unaware of our condition. It appears that apathy — the lack of emotion or interest — has filled our nation spiritually.

In this year of 2016 when Americans are preparing for a presidential election in November, both political parties are divided between themselves. My son, Bryan, said it best by describing our leaders across our land as those who were living at the beginning of the tower of Babel. Because of their ignorance, God confounded the language of all the earth to the point that they could not understand one another's speech (Hosea 4). Does this not sound like America? Even in our churches, we find so much confusion and unrest. Just listen to the news media and you will hear of so many proclaiming that America should stop supporting the nation of Israel. Alcohol is flowing like a river. Gambling is now a popular trend. Policemen are being portrayed as criminals. A number of (so-called) churches are promoting sodomy. Couples have decided to just live together, commit fornication, adultery and the like without any fear of consequences.

A number of megachurches have great crowds of people who are expecting to come as they are and leave as they were. My daughter was invited to a cell group meeting of a family from such a church. After arrival, the host family brought out their beer, explaining that there would be those attending who desire alcohol with their meal. The church has become so worldly minded that lost people feel comfortable being lost; they see no difference between themselves and the church members. Many churches have become so worldly that there is little time and effort spent in the Word of God.

Worship is so important in the growth of the church. However, there is no true worship if the Word of God is simply placed on the shelf. America is reaping what it has sown. We have traded faith for a frolic and biblical education for entertainment. As in Hosea's day, our desire has bent toward idolatry and lovers of pleasure more than lovers of God. What happened then is now happening in our day. Because of our self-dependency without the Bible, churches are dying for lack of knowledge. As goes the church, so goes the nation. The people in Hosea's day were not being exterminated or consumed; rather, their spiritual force was destroyed. These people of God had lost their influence and respect because believers compromised with the world. Instead of turning to God, they turned to idols. These rejected the Word of God by ignoring God's Word.

When there is a neglect of the Word of God, our behavior becomes careless, churches become powerless, and God-favored people begin to falter. When the church begins to falter, our dedication begins to cease. Are we so blind today that we cannot see this truth? Is there no answer for our dilemma? Yes, there is! It is found in Hosea 6:1-2: "Come, and let us return unto the Lord; for He hath torn and He will heal us; He hath smitten and He will bind us up, and we shall live in His sight."

For America to be revitalized, revitalization must begin in the church! We need to believe God's Word and exercise our faith in response to His Word. Philippians 4:19 promises us: "My God shall supply all your need according to his riches in glory in Christ Jesus." Yes, revitalization can be a reality, so take courage and go forward!

One of the most trying experiences I have faced in building up a church was after serving as pastor of Temple Baptist Church for thirteen years. At that time, I received a call from Delano McMinn concerning a new mission church that began in his house. While serving as director of missions for the Saluda Baptist Association, Delano had a deep desire to have a new church-start in a certain area in Anderson, South Carolina. At this time the mission was meeting in a store building behind a shopping center on Highway 28 bypass. When Delano called, he asked me to pray about coming over to Anderson to help build up this new mission work. After weeks of prayer, discussions with Delano, and meeting with the church's members, my wife, our daughter, Sherry, and I decided to go and help with this new work. My daughter had recently graduated from Southside Christian School, and she was so needed in this ministry.

The first Sunday, April 1, 2000, we began serving as their new pastor's family. There were fourteen members present for Sunday school in addition to the three of us. Here we were, with a grand total of seventeen people present. We had to travel forty-eight miles one way to the church. The grand total for the offering was around $500 weekly. Out of this weekly income, rent had to be paid, in addition to utilities, insurance, the pianist, and the secretary at $25 per week. Someway, somehow, God would provide for my family, as well. My daughter cried after she realized our family would be separated for the first time, with my two sons and their families remaining at Temple Baptist Church in Simpsonville.

I realize that this new mission work was not revitalization, but a new church start. However, the same principles are needed in order to have the church moving forward in building Bible fellowship. This turned out to be a most exciting adventure, because we all were able to witness the manifestation of God. During the first few weeks, a ministry/dream team was established. A 20/20 vision was drawn up, with Sunday school being a top priority, because this enhances Bible fellowship. Outside of this building were two metal buildings. One was for the children's ministry, and the other was for the youth. The first problem was that there were no children attending, and only two or three young people, and there were no teachers!

What would we do now? We decided to exercise our faith and claim God's Word. He tells us in His Word that if we had the faith as a grain of mustard seed, we could remove mountains. Our step of faith was to have a "Baby and Children's Shower," gathering needs for this area to prepare ourselves for growth. Before the day of the shower, everything we had listed had already been purchased. A great need that we had was for a minister of worship to be found. After making this a matter of prayer, Delano McMinn called and said that he had a résumé to cross his desk from someone who needed to be bi-vocational. After receiving this information, I called this brother in Christ, and we decided to meet together with our wives at a restaurant. When we met, I shared with this couple about our small income, but I promised to do what I could to raise at least $150 weekly for them to come. We had discussed doctrine, faithfulness, cooperation and faith, believing that God would provide. I explained my calling to this work and that we had so little to offer them. The couple said they would go home and pray over the matter. The following Sunday, as we began our worship service, Jerry and Phyllis Webster, the couple I had interviewed, walked in. After the service, they asked if I would meet with them again for dinner.

Bless God, at that dinner, they shared their testimonies and their desire to serve the Lord. They looked forward to serving with us and stated they would need no income to serve. My response was that we would give the amount promised, and if they wanted to give it elsewhere they should do so. Jerry was not only a gifted worship minister and a great partner in ministry, his wife, Phyllis, was an excellent musician. God manifested Himself, assuring us of His presence and help. Within only a few weeks, another couple visited our mission work. As they were leaving, speaking to our ministry team, they informed us of their church's closing, and they were giving us first choice to purchase their facilities. We had already agreed on locating on Highway 81 if property ever became available, and here was property only about two miles from that location. But how could we purchase this with so little income?

When our leaders visited the property, there was a building, worship center, baptismal pool, Sunday school classrooms, a small kitchen and fellowship hall, a piano, keyboard, organ, choir area, office furniture, copier, computer appliances, pews and sound equipment. Outside was a twenty-by-twenty utility building, tractor, bush hog, lawn mower, weed eaters — and all of this was on over eight acres of land. When we inquired about the asking price, it was only around $9,500 — for everything! God manifested Himself again!

While in the process of closing out the property and making arrangements to relocate, I overheard someone telling of a young man at their workplace who had surrendered to full-time Christian service. I asked if the young man might want to come and serve as our minister of youth. A few days later, he called me, and we set up an appointment to meet. Again, I had to explain that we had so little to offer. As far as finances were concerned, I shared that we would try to give at least $150 weekly to help him with gas and eats. He had stated that he would like to be bi-vocational, and he did not have to receive anything. Here we go again! God blessed us with Joel and Dora Keown and their five children! What another gift from God! God will continue to manifest Himself when we humble ourselves, die to ourselves, stand on God's Word and exercise our faith.

With confidence, this mission, Sierra Baptist Church, began to put the Sunday school together. I trust that you, the reader, will follow along, because these principles will work anywhere. Church renewal and revitalization is a thrilling experience. It is stepping out into the unknown, knowing that God will never leave us nor forsake us; according to His Word, He will supply all of our needs.

Now let us turn our attention to the Sunday school. Where do we start? With only a handful of people, a nucleus, we start where we are and with those who are with us. In all of the situations I have been in, there has always been someone present whom God has used to keep the nucleus together. When the nucleus begins praying, preaching, teaching, visiting, writing letters, making phone calls and believing, God always rewards our efforts when all is done for His glory. After becoming the pastor of this small mission church, I began praying. My wife and I started a new young adult Sunday school class. My wife loved making calls, sending cards and visiting to help reach others for Christ. My daughter can sing so well, and she has been a great partner in our ministry. Besides all of this, God has always manifested Himself by sending the right people at the right time to help fulfill the needs we had. He will do the same for you.

Again we must remember Proverbs 29:18: "Where there is no vision, the people perish." In order to catch a great vision, keep in mind also Proverbs 27:27: "Iron sharpeneth iron." If we are to advance, we acknowledge God by asking Him to lead us to those who can help us. God has those within His kingdom's work who are ready, willing and able to assist us. In my case, there have always been those God would lay upon my heart over the years who helped me. First, there was my older, retired pastor, Rev. Dallas Suttles. He was an inspiration to me as a prayer partner and spiritual advisor. There was Aubert Rose, who has taught me over the years how to build up a Sunday school and how to deal with problem churches. Dr. Harold Hunter, former pastor of the First Baptist Church of North Jacksonville Baptist Church, became such a mentor to me, as he would come and preach revivals. He not only preached, but also, when asked, gave such wonderful advice that always helped the church where I pastored. After becoming the president of Trinity College of the Bible and Trinity Theological Seminary, he was always there to pray, help and encourage me whenever there was a need.

Following in his steps was his son, Braxton Hunter. As I began to grow older, Braxton became a very successful young pastor who knew how to preach, win souls and build a church. With the anointing of God, this young man later entered the evangelism field, preaching all over the country and in other parts of the world. Whenever he came to preach in revival, crowds would always come and souls would be saved. Now, having become the new president at Trinity, Braxton is able to help not only me but hundreds of others working throughout God's kingdom.

Proverbs 13:20 advises us: "He that walketh with wise men shall be wise; but a companion of fools shall be destroyed." With Aubert Rose being such a wise man in his field of service — that of knowing how to build a Sunday school — I would invite him about every two years to preach, teach, train and challenge the congregation where I was serving. What he shared with me, I want to pass on to you.

In one of our first meetings, Aubert explained to us "Seven Principles for Church Growth." From that time on, these principles have been applied to the ministry where I served. Before a congregation is revitalized, the leadership needs to know where they are going. The following are these principles.

First, there must be an objective. In other words, what is our aim? What is our purpose, and what are we striving for? The answer is found in Matthew 28:19-20. These were the last words of our Lord Jesus as He was going away, leaving His Great Commission to His disciples. This was not just to be read, but to be put into practice! Here is where we begin: "And Jesus came and spake unto them, saying, All power is given unto Me in heaven and in earth. Go ye therefore and teach all nations, baptizing them in the name of the Father, and of the Son and of the Holy Ghost; teaching them to observe all things whatsoever I have commanded you; and, lo, I am with you always, even unto the end of the world." This is our objective in revitalizing our churches. It is like the plan of salvation. It is so simple to understand. Today, many think that because we have a good location, a beautiful facility, a great entertainment center and a whole lot of activities, everyone should be coming to our churches. My friend, that is not God's plan. We must first begin with the words of Jesus and "Go tell." Let us put feet to our prayers. Let us be about our Father's business — making disciples, marking disciples and maturing disciples.

Second, there must be a motivation. Our motivation comes from 1 Corinthians 9:24: "Know ye not that they which run in a race run all, but one receiveth the prize? So run that ye may obtain." If we are to experience our church being revitalized, then we cannot just sit there like the "frozen chosen" and mourn over a church that is dying. Instead, let us rise up and get on with what God has told us to do! We have God's command, God's instruction, and also His promise that He would be with us always!

Third, there must be a desire. Honestly, what is your desire? Is it to have just enough people in your church to pay the bills and to settle for the status quo? Or is it inspired by God as the Apostle Paul, in Romans 10:1, who confessed: "Brethren, my heart's desire and prayer to God is that they might be saved." When we as leaders and members have such a desire, God will revitalize such a church.

Fourth, there must be faith. The Apostle Paul said, "I can do all things through Christ which strengtheneth me" (Philippians 4:13). In my last pastorate, this verse of scripture was placed on our overhead screen in order for everyone to see and to read it together. We must not only talk about faith, we must exercise our faith. Hebrews 11:6 is very clear: "But without faith it is impossible to please Him; for they that cometh to God must believe that He is, and that He is a rewarder of them that diligently seek Him."

Fifth, we must be willing to work. In John 9:4, Jesus said, "I must work the works of Him that sent Me, while it is day; the night cometh, when no man can work." Building up a church, reaching souls for Christ, preaching and teaching God's Word, and being about our Father's business involves work! Yet it is the most joyful, fulfilling and rewarding work in this old world. There is no greater joy than to know you are working for the King of kings and Lord of lords!

Sixth, there must be a program. A plan of action is needed. Where is a plan to follow? I suggest you read Deuteronomy 31:12-13. Here is an Old Testament text explaining a program that works! Today we call this Sunday school, Bible study, or cell groups. "Gather the people together, men, women, children and thy stranger that is within thy gates, that they may hear, and that they may learn and fear the Lord your God, and observe to do all the words of this law. And that their children which have not known anything, may hear and learn to fear the Lord your God." I am personally sold on Sunday school, Bible study and/or cell groups if the purpose involves carrying out God's plan of action. Here is real revitalization within the church!

Seventh, there must be an evaluation. This is based on Luke 10:17-21. In this passage of scripture we find our Lord sending out seventy of His followers, two by two, into every city and place. He informed them, "The harvest truly is great, but the labourers are few; pray ye therefore the Lord of the harvest, that He would send forth labourers into His harvest" (verses 1-2). When the seventy returned, they "did so with joy, saying, Lord, even the devils are subject unto us through Thy name." In other words, souls were coming to Christ, lives were being changed. In verse 21 we are told, "In that hour Jesus rejoiced in spirit." I am sure Jesus rejoiced many times in His life, but take note that this is the only verse of scripture where it is written, "Jesus rejoiced!" My friend, if you want joy to return to your church and if you want real church revitalization to take place in your midst, you have just read how it can take place. Why not take an evaluation of your church right now?

These are principles that work. I pray that you will implement them within your church as soon as possible and begin to rejoice! As you look closely at Deuteronomy 31:12-13, you will notice the gathering of men, women, children, and strangers. As you begin to reach out to others, God will begin "little by little" to draw out teachers. Someone will teach the men. Another will rise up and teach the ladies. Another will have a desire to reach the youth and the children. Someone will have a burden to go to the fields and compel others to come. All of this will happen as you continue faithfully with these principles. God will manifest Himself, and you will become more excited about the cause of Christ than ever before. Your best days may be right in front of you!

Another great man of God who influenced my life and ministry is a man I have never met in my life, nor have I heard him speak at any conference. This man was known as "Mr. Sunday School." His name was Leon Kilbreth. It was a miracle of God as to how I came to know about him. It was back in the 1980s and '90s. It was right after I became the pastor of Temple Baptist Church. This was the church where I faced the greatest testing in my ministry. Remember what the Apostle Paul said: "But my God shall supply all of your need according to his riches in glory by Christ Jesus" (Philippians 4:19). This is exactly what happened as soon as I became pastor of this troubled church.

Pastor Bobby Lindsey gave me a copy of a Leon Kilbreth series on video. One of the series was on the subject, "Why Churches Stop Growing." When I viewed this message, I realized that this should be seen by our church members. To the churches that are struggling and in a decline, this would be so valuable in 2016. As a result of showing this to our congregation, a large number of our people began to repent and confess our need to return totally to Christ and to His Word. God began transforming this congregation because of the message of the video. Leon Kilbreth, a man I never met, was used of God to turn this church around. In summary, here is what he shared.

The reasons why churches stop growing are six-fold:

1) There is a lack of burden. We have elected deacons, teachers and other leaders who have no burden for reaching the lost. They talk about it and say they are concerned, but, by their actions, they really do not have a burden for souls. Since viewing his message,

I have noticed there are very, very few deacons and teachers who ever participate in the outreach ministry of the church. Why? Because they lack a burden.

2) There is a fear of failure. Many fear the future and stepping out on childlike faith. Therefore, the church becomes dormant and defeated.

3) Leaders become stagnant. Our churches become satisfied and comfortable, with no expectations. The church becomes dull and boring.

4) There is an irresponsible leadership. When blind leaders lead the blind, they both will fall into the ditch — the ditch of apathy and numbness. No wonder so many churches are in a decline today.

5) There are overlooked opportunities. Look around our churches today. The mission field has come to the doorsteps of our churches. Our population is growing by leaps and bounds. There are more lost people around us now more than ever. With our facilities, modern technology and half-empty buildings, and with the Holy Spirit ready to assist us, opportunities to reach the lost and to grow the church are at our disposal! These can be the most exciting days in our lifetime. Pray for God to anoint our eyes with spiritual eye salve that we may see, and unplug our ears that we may hear, the golden opportunities before us! May many churches experience the joy of revitalization!

6) We ignore God's timetable. In John 4:35, we read the words of Jesus: "Say not ye, there are yet four months and then cometh the harvest? Behold, I say unto you, Lift up your eyes, and look on the fields; for they are white already to harvest."

My friend, the opportunities are at our fingertips. May our Lord stir our hearts again as we return to His Holy Word, and may we experience revitalization in our churches!

Chapter Review: Building Up Bible Fellowship

Hosea 4:6

Hosea 6:1-2; Philippians 4:19; Proverbs 27:27, 13:30

My mentors: Rev. Dallas Suttles, Rev. Charles Lavender, Dr. Harold Hunter, Aubert Rose, Rick Ingle, Delano McMinn, Leon Kilbreth

Seven Principles for Church Growth
>   There must be an *objective* (Matthew 28:19-20)
>   There must be a *motivation* (1 Corinthians 9:24)
>   There must be a *desire* (Romans 10:1)
>   There must be *faith* (Philippians 4:13; Hebrews 11:6)
>   We must be willing to *work* (John 9:4)
>   There must be a *program* (Deuteronomy 31:12-13)
>   There must be an *evaluation* (Luke 10:17-21)

Six Reasons Why Churches Stop Growing
>   There is a lack of burden
>   There is a fear of failure
>   Leaders become stagnant
>   Irresponsible leadership
>   Overlooked opportunities
>   We ignore God's timetable

Chapter Eleven

Transitioning to Ministries

And he gave some, apostles; and some, prophets; and some, evangelists; and some, pastors and teachers; For the perfecting of the saints, for the work of the ministry, for the edifying of the body of Christ. (Ephesians 4:11-12)

This is one chapter I would like for every church member to read! Have you ever served on a search committee to seek out a pastor for a church? It is truly a learning experience. Usually, after a meeting is planned, someone begins the meeting with a prayer. The prospective pastor is asked to give his testimony. In most cases, there is a discussion about the pastor's family, his education, his goals and plans. His education is explained, along with his call to the ministry and his doctrinal beliefs. Somewhere within the meeting, everyone gives their own opinion on the responsibility of the pastor. There are opinions about preaching, teaching, discipling, hospital visitation, nursing home visitation, homebound visitation, witnessing, weekly visitation, and on and on. There are so many demands placed on the pastor that are not scriptural. Many churches plan to hire a preacher to do the work of the ministry. During the first two or three years after a pastor is called, there is the "Kitty, kitty" stage. During the next two or three years there is the "Poor kitty" stage, and then, after that, it is the "Scat, cat, you rascal, you" stage. If we aren't careful, we can make our churches become so strictly organized by placing so many demands upon the pastor and a certain few within the church that we lose our joy of service.

I remember the first committee I was asked to serve with. It was the nominating committee. By being on that committee, I was asked by its members to serve on the counting committee. There were about six to eight members on the nominating committee scheduling our future meetings, as we would seek out members who would be willing to serve in a particular area for a three-year period, after which they would rotate off. It wasn't long after I had served in this capacity that someone told me he believed that a camel was a horse designed by a Baptist committee. After becoming a pastor and witnessing some who had been chosen to serve in positions, I almost believed that statement!

Think about our churches for a moment. A group of members called the nominating committee is set aside to seek out workers within the church. They pray over the workers, and then go out to ask people to serve in different areas of the church. Due to our little finite minds, we keep placing the same old crowd to continue doing what it has always been doing, and the church ends up in a rut! When the nominating committee assigned me to approach a certain individual to serve within a certain committee, he simply replied, "No." He was not at all interested. So, back to the drawing board we went. It took a while to find someone to fill that position, and also several more meetings. It was amazing how much time was wasted when we could have been about our Father's business, accomplishing something more worthwhile.

So we have a handful of people serving on a committee who do not know the hearts, the spiritual gifts nor the desires of most of our church members. Most of the time when we have our other committees in place, there are usually only a few of those who actually do the work. Besides all of this, think about how many more church members we have who are never asked to serve anywhere!

Look carefully at Ephesians 4:11-12. The scripture tells us that God has placed apostles, prophets, evangelists, pastors and teachers within the church. You read of nothing concerning hospitals, nursing homes, visitation, custodial work, buildings, grass cutting, etc. What God's Word is saying here is that those leaders whom God has placed within the church have a threefold responsibility.

First, they are to "perfect the saints." The goal of the pastor and staff is to mature the saints. How is this done? It is through the Word of God. Most Christians have no clue what a spiritual gift is; therefore, they do not know what they can do within the church. Most church members have "joined" the church and think they have reached the promised land. These members may love the church, but they are missing out on so many blessings through service for our Lord. For years, I always thought the preacher was the one "called" into the ministry. How many times have we heard it said that a certain person has been "called" to preach? Yes, he may have been called, but the preacher/pastor is not the only one called to minister. We are all called to ministry. My ministry is preaching, teaching, evangelizing and serving — and I love the ministry!

The second responsibility of the pastor is to allow the members to serve. When the leadership of the church "perfects the saints," the members can "do the work of the ministry." They will not only know how to do the work, they will also want to work because this will be God's work — working for the King! After perfecting (maturing) the saints, and with the saints doing the work of the ministry, the church is edified — that is, built up! We are told in verses 15-16: "But speaking the truth in love, may grow up into Him in all things, which is the head, even Christ; from whom the whole body fitly joined together and compacted by that which every joint supplieth, according to the effectual working in the measure of every part, making increase of the body unto the edifying of itself in love."

The third responsibility is to edify the church. God wants His church to grow up. He wants to see us make "increase in the body" and "to edify" the church in love. This is accomplished when we grow spiritually. "As newborn babes," we are to "desire the sincere milk of the Word, that [we] may grow thereby." If we will seek to grow spiritually, we will grow numerically. Let us "go" and "grow." It is like breathing. When we "grow," we will "go." Remember: "For God so loved the world that He gave His only begotten son that whosoever believeth in Him will not perish but have everlasting life" (John 3:16). May our love for Christ and for sinners cause us to "go into all the world, and preach the gospel to every creature" (Mark 16:15). "Go out into the highways and hedges, and compel them to come in, that My house may be filled" (Luke 14:23). If we will grow spiritually, we will grow numerically, and if we grow numerically, we will grow financially. God promised to supply all of our needs.

There, within your church, God has already begun to provide for you. You are one of God's gifts to the church if you know Jesus as your Lord and Savior. When we, the leaders of the church, perfect the saints to do the work of the ministry, a third thing will take place: The body of Christ will be edified. That is, the church will be built up and Jesus will be glorified. When Christ is glorified, the church will experience revitalization!

When you look out through your congregation, whether your church is large or small, there are people around you whom God has gifted to help edify the church. What has been so encouraging to me is to see those who never thought they would be used of God become motivated servants in the church. This is my joy in ministry. By going through a "committee" mentality, we limit God. Most church members have no idea what to do or how to do ministry. These same people would like to serve in some area, but the committee never asks them. A committee is limited. We only know our closest friends and relatives. So what about the other gifted people in the church?

Transitioning to ministries is a simple process and involves many more believers for service. For this to be accomplished, we need to understand the purpose of making this transition. The purpose is to educate all of our members so that the preacher will not be the only minister. We are all ministers!

When certain ones are asked to serve on a committee, this is a good thing. For years and years, by the process of a committee, we have grown denominations and churches and built many organizations. There are some areas where only a few may have any knowledge of how to serve. But, by transitioning to ministries, more members will be able to serve, train and teach others. Every church member should realize that he or she has gifts and abilities to be used in edifying the church.

Let me share with you a few ways I have discovered to make this transition. One way to begin is by simply recommending that the wording in your bylaws be changed from committee to ministry. In other words, your church would call the building and grounds committee the building and grounds ministry. Replace the word "committee" everywhere by changing it to a ministry. Begin immediately educating your church concerning ministry. Everyone can have a part in ministry. This is so simple, yet so powerful, in that it motivates every believer to become a minister in service. I started trying to implement such a procedure while pastoring Temple Baptist Church in the 1980s. I wasn't very successful, because I had a difficult time adjusting to so many things.

When I began working with the new ministry in Anderson, South Carolina, there were no bylaws. As soon as I became pastor, we began organizing ministries — instead of committees — as part of our 20/20 vision. We wanted everyone who became a member of our church to fill out a ministry sheet that listed the possible areas of ministries. We asked each member to sign up for three to five areas where he or she would like to serve. Anyone who wished to serve with children, youth or finance were required to have a background check. We also realized what the Bible tells us about leadership in 2 Timothy 2:2: "And the things that thou hast heard of one among many witnesses, the same commit thou to faithful men, who shall be able to teach others also." Proverbs 25:19 warns: "Confidence in an unfaithful man in time of trouble is like a broken tooth and a foot out of joint." At the time of service, with a new ministry and with no deacons, our ministry team and pastor took all the names of those who had signed up for different ministries and prayed over those names. We then placed the names under the ministries in which they had interest. From the names, we chose faithful chairpersons to be placed over the different ministries. The chairperson then called all of those listed under that ministry to organize and plan out their responsibilities and goals for the church year. This was done during the month of May in order for everything to be in place by the first of September, when our new church year began.

On the following pages, you will be given an idea to begin a plan of action. Remember, this was the beginning of a new ministry with only seventeen people present in our first service. By preparing this simple sheet of paper, the ministries grew and, before long, we had all positions filled. This sheet of paper is what we called our "mustard seed faith." As the result of this one sheet of paper, God blessed our faith, and more ministries were later added.

There is one thing I have come to realize through this process in all the places God called me. Every situation was different, and there were different needs, but God always gave us exactly the right people to serve when the need arose!

This new mission work is a great example of how to begin in a church that needs revitalization. We only had a $500 per week offering. In spite of this, within the first nine months we had purchased over eight acres of land with all the facilities and furnishings we would need. The financial needs were also met. God also supplied a minister of worship, two fine musicians, a minister of students and an associate pastor. The main quote around this new church was, "This is a God thing!"

Let us look carefully at the "committee" way of doing things and transitioning to a "ministries" model. With committees, we spend so much time with meetings. We first have to approve a list of names for the nominating committee. This committee then meets to begin organizing not one, but several meetings over an extended amount of time. During the first meeting, the needs of the church are reviewed from the previous year. If there is a need for a new committee, it will be added. For the next several days, the nominating committee will be thinking of names of those who might serve for a three-year period before rotating off. At the next meeting, these names will be reviewed and discussed. Meetings like this generally last for some two hours, at least. By the end of the meeting, the names of those the committee agree upon will be divided between the nominating committee members to be contacted. The prospective names of those contacted usually agree to serve or not serve, or they will ask for time to pray about it.

Usually, most of those contacted will serve, but there are always some who will not. Therefore, this will call for another meeting (or two). This particular meeting involves soul-searching and become somewhat desperate because there has to be a certain number listed, according to the bylaws. Most of the time, at least one more meeting will be needed in order to finalize the report. When the nominating committee completes its report, it is then printed and presented to the church for approval. Now think for a moment. It will have taken not several weeks, but several months to complete such a report and have it approved. At the same time, think about the number of church members who were never considered and were never asked about serving anywhere. Our little finite minds cannot comprehend the many members who would serve in some area if they only knew what was available for them and if they were challenged to minister in some area.

Let us now turn our attention to the "ministries" method of service. If every member had the opportunity to sign up for a possibility of service, it would be much simpler, and a larger number of saints of God could serve! The best example of this would be found at Laurel Baptist Church. Here is the church that dropped in attendance to around thirty people in Sunday school and worship. This was about four and a half years ago. Today, this same church has some forty different ministries!

Below, you will find an overview of some of the ministries that are in place. A listing of the ministries is provided for everyone who is a member of the church who may desire to sign up to serve. During the month of May, the goal of the church is to have all positions filled. This is so exciting and motivating for the entire church.

Discipleship Ministry
    Men's Ministry
    New Member Orientation
    Women's Ministry
    Training for Special Ministries
    Counselors

Education Ministry
    Adult Sunday School Teachers/Leaders
    Bulletin Boards
    Church Calendars
    Church Directory
    Historian
    Homebound Sunday School
    Library
    Tuesday AM Bible Study

Evangelism Ministry
    FAITH Witnessing Training
    FAITH Meals
    Marketing
    Social Media
    Website
    Telethon

Music Ministry
    Choir
    Ensemble
    Instruments
    Audio
    Visual

Fellowship Ministry
  Decorations/Flowers
  DOTS (Dining Out Together Somewhere)
  Events
  Photographer
  Staff Encouragement
  Tables/Chairs/Trash
  Wedding Coordinator
  Young at Heart

Financial Ministry
  Stewardship
  Tellers
  Treasurer (appointed position)

Hispanic Ministry
  Discipleship
  Mission Opportunities/Trips
  Outreach

Missions Ministry
  Bereavement Meals
  Eastside Crisis Center
  Laurel Ringers (Ministry to Nursing Homes)
  Mission Projects
  Mission Trips

Prayer Ministry
  Hospital
  Shut-in
  Prayer

Operations Ministry
  Building
  Electrical
  Plumbing
  Painting

Cemetery
Grounds
Office Volunteers
Safety
Sign
Transportation/Trips

Preschool/Children/Youth Ministry
AWANA
Children
Children's Church
Extended Session
Preschool
VBS
Youth
Youth Equipping the Saints

Worship Ministry
Baptism Preparation
Lord's Supper Preparation
Ushers
Welcome

Personnel Ministry (filled)
Pastor
Minister of Education
Minister of Students
Minister of Music
Minister to Hispanics
ACTS Director
Deacon Chairman

Remember, these areas of service were filled within a month simply by making the list of ministries needed for the coming year. This number of ministries was not completed in the first year, but grew over a four-year period. If this can happen with Laurel Baptist Church, when they nearly had to close their facilities four years ago, it can also become a reality within your church.

When the names are gathered together, the deacons and pastor will pray over and review the names, select a ministry chairperson for each area of service, meet with the chairpersons, and prepare the people for service. There are two things you should consider. First, this does not consume months of your time with endless meetings. Second, it is better to have more people involved in service who truly want to serve! It is much more exciting to see those who have never served in the church become servants for their Lord than to have them sitting on a pew while a handful of dedicated members are doing everything!

Ephesians 4:4-6 informs us: "There is one body, and one spirit, even so ye are called in one hope of your calling; one Lord, one faith, one baptism, one God and Father of all, who is above all, and through all, and in all." God is in us all! We are all called into this hope of our calling! In verse 7, we find it very clear: "But unto every one of us is given grace according to the measure of the gift of Christ." Every one of us received God's grace — not a select few — but all who receive Christ as Savior and Lord. As a result of our faith in Jesus Christ, "He gave some, apostles; and some, prophets; and some, evangelists and some, pastors and teachers (verse 11). Why did He specifically point out these leaders within the church? The answer is found in verse 12: "For the perfecting of the saints, for the work of the ministry, for the edifying of the body of Christ." God's plan and purpose for leadership of the church is to "perfect the saints," that is, to mature the saints, to teach them, all of them, to do "the work of the ministry." When members are trained to do the work of the ministry, the pastor will not be expected to visit every nursing home or every member who is in the hospital, nor to do all the visiting.

There are those within your membership who will help your church as the result of prayer. They will become disciples for the work of the ministry. The body of Christ — the church — will be edified! The church will grow spiritually, numerically and financially. Pray for God to open our eyes to see this truth. Some of them have been given special abilities: to some apostles; to others the gift of preaching; some have special abilities to win people to Christ, helping them to trust in Christ as their Savior; to others a gift of caring for the sheep as a shepherd cares; and to some the gift of leading and teaching them in the ways of God.

God's people will be equipped to do a good work for Christ, building up the church, the body of Christ. The church will be strengthened and matured until we become more and more like Christ, who is the Head of His body, the Church. Through Christ's direction, the whole body will be fitted together, and each part, in its own special way, will help the other parts of the body so that the church will be healthy, growing, and full of love!

These basic principles will work anywhere if you will pray over them, exercise faith and, little by little, believe you can take your mountain. You can — with God's help and by following God's Word. Let me encourage you to pray about transitioning from committees to ministries.

Chapter Review: Transitioning to Ministries

Ephesians 4:11-2

The leadership:
    Perfects (matures) the saints
    Involves the members
    Builds up the church

The committee:
    Limits the workers
    Lowers expectations
    Hides the possibilities
    Wastes time

The ministry:
    Makes disciples (2 Timothy 2:2)
    Multiplies workers
    Enlightens the membership
    Equips the Body of Christ

Chapter Twelve

PROMOTING MISSIONS MORE EFFECTIVELY

And Judah said, "The strength of the bearers of burdens is decayed, and there is much rubbish; so that we are not able to build the wall." (Nehemiah 4:10)

One of the great blessings of God is to have been raised in and around a Southern Baptist church. As a result of this experience, I have been able to hear so much about missions. From the time I was a little boy, the importance of missions has been promoted in so many ways. Over the years, Southern Baptists have promoted the Janie Chapman, Annie Armstrong, and Lottie Moon Christmas offerings, offerings for world hunger, and several other missions, as well. Giving for different causes has always been emphasized in order to spread the gospel throughout the world.

We have been taught: "For with the heart man believeth unto righteousness; and with the mouth confession is made unto salvation. For the scripture saith, whosoever believeth on Him shall not be ashamed" (Romans 10:11-12). As believers we have come to understand, "For whosoever shall call upon the name of the Lord shall be saved" (Romans 10:13).

Missions, missions, missions has been promoted by our denomination because there is a realization that in order for souls to be saved, the gospel must be preached beyond our stained-glass windows and our Jerusalem. In order for this to happen, there must be a preacher willing to go to the fields, and there must be those who are willing to send the preacher. This is what missions is all about. "How then shall they call on him in whom they have not believed; and how shall they believe in whom they have not heard; and how shall they hear without a preacher; and how shall they preach except they be sent? As it is written, how beautiful are the feet of them that preach the gospel of peace, and bring glad tidings of good things" (Romans 10:14-15).

To experience the joy of church revitalization, we should remember the last words of our Lord Jesus before he departed for heaven: "Even unto the end of the world" (Matthew 28:20b). Church revitalization will be a reality when we understand that which we are doing is not all about us within the church walls; rather, we are to tell the wonderful story of Christ's death, burial and resurrection to the untold multitudes of people who have never heard the good news of the gospel. The church of the Lord Jesus is called to tell what has been seen and heard. We are to tell what actually happened according to the scripture.

We have come to understand the Great Commission, but we should also experience the grand submission! "Therefore they that were scattered abroad went everywhere preaching the Word" (Acts 8:4). If we are going to revitalize our church, let us be motivated by knowing we are a chosen people by the Word of God! "For ye see your calling, brother, how that not many wise after the flesh, not many mighty, not many noble are called; but God hath chosen the foolish things of the world to confound the wise; and God hath chosen the weak things of the world to confound the things which are might; and base things of the world, and things which are despised hath God chosen, yea, and things which are not, to bring to nothing things that are" (1 Corinthians 1:26-28). Notice the word "ye." God has chosen us, ordinary men and women, boys and girls, to be witnesses. Consider your church. Do you see how God can do a work within your church that may seem so insignificant and helpless to bring glory to His name? Does the scripture from Acts 1:8 excite, challenge and encourage you and your church when you read the promise from our Lord Jesus Christ: "But ye shall receive power, after that the Holy Ghost is come upon you; and ye shall be witnesses unto me both in Jerusalem, and in all Judea, and in Samaria, and unto the uttermost part of the earth" (Acts 1:8)?

Meditate on this verse! God has chosen you and your church to be witnesses for our Lord. He has not chosen Superman to accomplish this task. He has chosen the foolish things, the base things, the weak things, to carry out His will. He promises to empower you! God can take you and your church and make you a witness in your community, in your city, in your country and beyond the confines of our imagination! God used one deacon by the name of Philip, who faced deep-seated racial and religious prejudices in Samaria, when none of the others were willing to submit. As a result, revival broke out in Samaria. Eventually the other apostles went there!

Revitalization is a result of our willingness to submit to going and telling the good news of the gospel everywhere! But we must begin where we are. The Holy Spirit has been given to us to enable us to obey the Lord's command in witnessing effectively for Him. We have a job to do, an assignment to fulfill. We must be about our Father's business immediately. Time is short, the need is great, the matter is urgent, millions are lost, and the laborers are few. Do not just sit there. Rise up and take action! God has promised never to leave you or forsake you. He is ready to help you. Will you submit to His will? Be encouraged, because revitalization can become a reality within your church. But it must begin with you!

Perhaps you and your church feel like the Apostle Paul when he wrote: "We are troubled on every side, yet not distressed, we are perplexed, but not in despair; persecuted, but not forsaken; cast down, but not destroyed" (2 Corinthians 4:8-9). You and your church may be confronting some problems that many men of God have experienced throughout history. You have just read two verses of scripture whereby you can find comfort. God has not forgotten you or your church. When Nehemiah was called by

God and commissioned by the king to rebuild the wall of Jerusalem, he secured others who would help accomplish this mission. Nehemiah faced all kinds of discouragements, and we can learn from them.

Here was a man who was called and equipped for his journey to Jerusalem. He had prayed earnestly and was surrounded by a great host of people who were ready to help. It wasn't long before Sanballat, Tobiah and Geshem rose in opposition as the enemies of God's people. The devil will not give up without a fight, but, praise God, in Nehemiah's day, His people had a mind to work. Opposition is to be expected any time we submit ourselves to the lordship of Christ and begin afresh to do his will. Yes, this is to be expected, but what is just as discouraging is to have those among our fellowship fighting against rebuilding the wall and revitalizing our church. Imagine: Judah, of all people, approaches Nehemiah and says, "The strength of burdens is decayed, and there is much rubbish; so that we are not able to build the wall." What happened to Judah? He was sorely grieved at the ruins of the great city. You have perhaps seen on television where places in the Middle East, such as Syria, Lebanon and elsewhere, have been bombed and destroyed. Buildings were leveled to the ground, and roads no longer existed. In Nehemiah's day, the city of Jerusalem, including her gates, had been destroyed. Nehemiah had already seen the destruction, and he had wept over the ruins in the night.

Does this not seem similar to your situation? You enter your worship center, your parking lot, your Sunday school classrooms, and you see an emptiness where a spiritual destruction has taken place. When Nehemiah saw the ruins of this great city, he rose to the task of rebuilding the wall. What about you? Will you rise to the task before you? Will you ask God about what you can do? If the walls of Jerusalem could be rebuilt as the result of one man — Nehemiah, who had such a burden — can you not believe God can use someone like you to rebuild the spiritual wall of your church?

Judah, like so many within our churches, saw rubbish everywhere.

He was just like the spies with Caleb and Joshua who saw the giants and discouraged the people, keeping many from entering the promised land. Caleb and Joshua, like Nehemiah, were ready to take God at His Word and go in to take the land. Judah told Nehemiah that the workers' desire to rebuild the wall was not there after seeing the sad situation and rubbish everywhere. Nehemiah knew beyond a shadow of a doubt that God had placed a burden upon his heart to rebuild the wall of Jerusalem. He had also witnessed the hand of God in opening this door of opportunity and supplying every need he had. There was no turning back for Nehemiah. He never considered for one moment turning back. He had been called of God. He had been given this open door, and he was willing to go alone. He knew God was with him! In any church that is desperate for revitalization, you will hear the pessimists and the doom-and-gloom people. Satan will have those inside the church as well as those on the outside who will hinder and seek to discourage those who want to believe God for revitalization.

Write the word "rubbish" in the front part of your Bible. The reason for this is because rubbish is all around churches that are in decline. It is now time for a Nehemiah in our day to have the burden of the Lord upon his heart to seek the Lord and believe God can assist in rebuilding the walls of our churches and bring about true revitalization! We already have our foundation, which is Jesus Christ alone. Let us now haul off the rubbish and rebuild!

As we consider promoting missions more effectively, I shared how my home church promoted the different special offerings. All of these offerings were taken in memory of very special servants of God over the years. Many churches, however, continue to take these offerings, remembering names like Janie Chapman, Annie Armstrong and Lottie Moon, reminding them of the mission. Yet missions giving hardly ever increases. In addition, we have a generation today that has no clue who these great missionaries were. There are those who talk about missions and have their studies about these fine missionaries, but some of this thinking has turned to rubbish. Don't get me wrong. Missions giving is good, and the studies are wonderful, but if we are serious about raising funds for missions, why not be willing to change our method of doing so?

I heard of a pastor who began serving with a different church. A certain lady who was a member of the church approached the pastor and began telling him how much she wanted the church to grow and how much she loved to visit. She then began telling this pastor about a recent visit she had. While visiting, she told a couple about the wonderful members in the church, then she asked the couple if they knew Janie Chapman. The couple responded, "No." She then asked them if they knew Annie Armstrong. Again the couple responded, "No." She could hardly believe what she was hearing! So she responded by saying to them, "Surely you know Lottie Moon!" To her surprise, they said to her, "We have never heard of these people." The lady said to them, "Well, you should start reading your Bible!"

This may seem somewhat comical, but this is the way it seems to be in some churches. Let me give you two examples. In a certain church where I pastored, there were many precious saints of God who were members there. Their Lottie Moon Christmas Offering goal was always $600 for the entire year. Here was a church where there were great people and great offerings. The problem was that they could not see far from their church and community. I tried to have them increase the offering to at least $1,000. For three or four months this offering was promoted. Yes, they had all their missions Bible studies, yet they could not see beyond their regular $600 yearly giving. Now this is rubbish! There needs to be a change in giving in such a church. The church could take up a love offering for a gospel-sing that would exceed the love offering given after a whole year for missions!

There was another wonderful church that had the same missions Bible studies with some forty ladies attending. They, too, decided to continue the old way of missions giving with their goal of $1,500. These precious ladies thought it would be best to keep their method of giving as it was. Today, after years have passed, you probably can guess what their yearly missions offering goal is! What are our churches doing? Are we serious about giving, or do we think these old methods of giving are written in the Bible?

Before becoming pastor of my last church, which was about to close its doors, I asked at the very beginning of my ministry to let us try something new. Instead of continually promoting one mission after another, I suggested we take one missions offering at the end of the year and call this our year-end Christmas offering. I encouraged them to set a goal of $5,000 and post this in the bulletin each Sunday beginning in January. This may seem like a small goal to your church if it has large numbers attending and if you have never faced the possible reality of closing your church doors. But to a church that has fallen to around thirty in Sunday school and has a total missions offering of only $1,800 for the entire previous year — which included the Annie Armstrong Easter Offering, the Janie Chapman Offering, the Lottie Moon Offering and other missions offerings — this looked like a mega offering to this church.

Everyone should understand that church revitalization involves more than taking up offerings, especially when a church is near closure. Church revitalization involves meetings, planning, organizing, much Bible study, prayer — and promoting missions is a part of the process!

A pastor cannot spend all of his time behind the pulpit addressing everyone's flowers, meetings, programs and announcements. Giving to missions is so important that we must not only talk about missions and study about missions, we are also to give to missions and do missions. At my last pastorate, with a large building that needed thousands of dollars of upgrades including heating and air units, renovating many of its facilities, improving sound systems, adding to staff needs, etc., missions had to be first. Keep in mind Matthew 6:33: "But seek ye first the kingdom of God and his righteousness and all these things shall be added unto you."

Luke 6:38 promises: "Give and it shall be given unto you; good measure, pressed down, and shaken together, and running over, shall men give unto your bosom. For with the same measure that ye mete withal it shall be measured to you again." Giving to missions is part of the church revitalization process. If we are to be blessed, we first begin by blessing others. One way to do this is by putting giving first!

Our first year together in my last pastorate was a wonderful learning experience for all of us. At the end of that first year, nearly $10,000 for missions was received, staff was added, some renovations were completed. Our dream team had developed a 20/20 vision, and because of the results of their faith in giving to missions and more to missions, the faith and hope in this church grew! To God be the glory!

Church revitalization is a rugged task. It takes faith, commitment and determination. If we are interested in the welfare of the church and have an ambition to please God, then we must be willing to adjust and throw out the rubbish that holds the church back. We do not see the rubbish because Satan has blinded our eyes when we do many good things but not the main thing. He does not care how busy we are, how many programs we have, how many announcements we make, as long as we do not concentrate on prayer, evangelism, discipleship, ministries, fellowship and worship! Let us throw out the rubbish!

Psalm 127:1 makes it very clear: "Except the Lord build the house, they labour in vain that build it." I am convinced, after thirty-seven years of pastoring, there are those who are members of a dying church who will do anything to keep the rubbish in the church. Signs could be placed throughout the church that read: "Don't touch this rubbish." There are those who will tell you how long they have been members, and they will tell you when all the good things happened years ago. However, they don't see themselves or their problem with hoarding rubbish. If anything stands in the way of revitalizing the church, reaching souls for Christ and growing God's kingdom, it is all rubbish!

In perhaps all churches there are those who speak clearly about how they want their church to grow. However, when it comes to new methods or ministries, you can listen and understand why the church is in such a decline. These people pray for growth and talk about growth, yet they do not want their "this or that" to be touched! They don't mind promoting social programs, entertaining and satisfying the flesh. If some of these are encouraged to try something new or to have someone else take their position, World War III will begin. Rubbish — this all rubbish!

Our Lord commanded us to make disciples. This was not a suggestion, but a command. Our Lord said, "Follow Me and I will make you fishers of men" (Matthew 4:19). If we who proclaim to be followers of Christ have held positions in the church for years and today have no one — absolutely no one — to fill our position, we have failed miserably at making disciples. We who are leaders within the church should constantly be seeking out someone to follow us as we follow Christ in order for that person (or persons) to take over when we step aside. This is exactly what the Apostle Paul did as he traveled from place to place. After a period of time in establishing a church, he would leave a Timothy or a Titus to carry on the work he began. Why then would anyone become angry and threaten to quit or leave their position, thinking their space has been encroached upon? I ask you, where is the person following you? Is there anyone prepared to take your place? Is there no one else qualified, or have you failed to train someone? Is it your space? The truth is, you have allowed this to become rubbish!

If a church is to experience revitalization, rubbish must go! We have our foundation, which is Jesus Christ our Lord, and His Word tells us to build upon this solid foundation. In 1 Corinthians 3:12, we are instructed clearly to build with gold, silver and precious stones; that is, we are to build upon that which fire cannot hurt, and we are to excavate the wood, hay and stubble — the rubbish. That which stands in the way of souls coming to Jesus is garbage and needs to be thrown out!

Alan Redpath's book, *Victorious Christian Service*, is a study in the book of Nehemiah. In regards to 1 Corinthians 3:12, he elaborates on the fact that in this verse our Lord is speaking not only about rubbish in the church, but rubbish in the heart of the Christian. Is this not the problem with our churches? Revitalization does not occur just because we have a building to meet in. First Corinthians 6:19 asks: "Know ye not that your body is the temple of the Holy Ghost?" If we are going to revitalize our church, we must first excavate, clear out the rubbish in our hearts, then deal with the facilities and other needs. The Apostle Paul said, "If any man defile the temple of God, him shall God destroy; for the temple of God is holy, which temple ye are." As I consider my life, I realize how little I have accomplished at times because of the rubbish of anger, temper, unbelief, pride, evil desire, self-importance, carelessness and a not-so-fruitful life over the years. God has blessed, but I am sure this temple of the Holy Spirit has been hindered because of the rubbish that has been there. When the blood of our Lord Jesus Christ was shed for me and I trusted him as my Lord and Savior, he came into my heart by the Holy Spirit of God. His power has been available, and He is willing to help me accomplish much for His glory. Yet, because of rubbish, so little has been accomplished.

Revitalization for the believer and for the church can be a reality, but we must deal with the rubbish in our churches and in our hearts. Three prescriptions are given by Alan Redpath that will help in revitalizing our churches.

The first is: Be sure that the foundation of your life is firmly laid. Be sure you stand on that foundation which no man can lay, which is Jesus Christ our Lord. Be sure you are not building on sinking sand. Be sure your faith is in Jesus Christ alone.

Second, remember that you are the temple of the Holy Spirit. Christ will build it. He began the work. He dug down and exposed your emptiness and threw out the self-righteousness and laid a solid foundation. Be sure you are saved — converted, not because you joined a particular church or were baptized or filled out a card at the church. Everything must be placed at the feet of Jesus Christ by trusting him and calling upon him alone. Remember, "Christ also loved the church, and gave himself for it; that he might sanctify and cleanse it with the washing of water by the Word. That he might represent it to himself a glorious church, not having spot or wrinkle, or any such thing; but that it should be holy and without blemish" (Ephesians 5:25-27).

Third, we are to build, for we are laborers together with God. I love how Alan Redpath words this: "We are to build this temple with all His power and all His strength and all His enabling." Second Peter 1:5-7 tells us how this is done: "Add to your faith virtue, and to virtue knowledge, and to knowledge temperance, and to temperance patience, and to patience godliness, and to godliness brotherly kindness, and to brotherly kindness charity."

Yes, Christ loved the church and gave Himself for it! Do you love the church? Does your faith rest in the blood of Jesus Christ? "For if these things be in you, and abound, they make you that ye shall neither be barren nor unfruitful in the knowledge of our Lord Jesus Christ" (2 Peter 1:8). Church revitalization can be a reality. It can begin with you. Begin anew by confessing your sin to God. God's Word promises: "If we confess our sins, He is faithful and just to forgive us our sins, and to cleanse us from all unrighteousness" (1 John 1:9).

My friend, God is able! Let us labor together in the church and build upon the solid foundation, which is Christ Jesus. He wants and is willing to help revitalize our churches. Let us throw out the rubbish in our hearts and lives.

I close with a quote from Alan Redpath: "The indwelling Christ is ready at the door of your heart to fill the garbage truck with all the rubbish that you are willing to get rid of, and by the grace of God and by the power of His Spirit, we will build the wall upon the foundation that will stand firm for time and eternity."

To this I say, "Amen!"

Chapter Review: Promoting Missions More Effectively

Nehemiah 4:10
Romans 10:11-15
1 Corinthians 1:26-28
Acts 1:8

Revitalization is a result of our willingness to submit to sharing
the gospel
   2 Corinthians 4:8-9
   This begins with you

Revitalization involves opposition and discouragement
   Nehemiah 4:10
   Sanballat, Tobiah, Geshem from without
   Judah and others from within

Revitalization demands clearing the rubbish
   Nehemiah 4:10
   Old ways that do not work
   Old sacred cows that are worshipped

Revitalization means putting first things first
   Matthew 6:33; Luke 6:38; Psalm 127:1
   The foundation is firmly laid
   Your body is the temple of the Holy Spirit
   We are laborers together

Chapter Thirteen

PLANNING A CHURCH REVITALIZATION CRUSADE

And they said, "Let us rise up and build." (Nehemiah 2:18)

It was in 1982 when Tony Smith, pastor of Bowman Baptist Church, invited me to travel with him to Athens, Georgia. He wanted us to hear Evangelist Aubert Rose, who would be preaching at Prince Avenue Baptist Church. I had just received a call to pastor my first full-time church in Iva, South Carolina. The population of Iva at that time was around 1,360 people, and my church was located some four miles outside of town, near the Georgia state line. From the city of Iva to the church, there were only nineteen houses along the way.

The reason for sharing this information with you is so you can understand what God did back then that set the stage for my ministry and what caused me to remain optimistic and excited about the churches God has allowed me to serve. As soon as I witnessed the gift that God had bestowed upon Aubert Rose, it was my desire to schedule him for the first revival crusade at my first full-time church.

My pastorate in Iva began in January 1983. The former pastor had served there for thirty-three years. He had a wonderful, successful ministry there, and everyone loved this dear pastor, Rev. Leroy Hayes, and his precious wife. Pastor Hayes was a graduate of Anderson College and one of our Southern Baptist seminaries. Now look what they were getting! For some reason, God saw fit for this church to call someone like me. I had not entered the ministry until I was almost thirty years of age, nor had

I received even an associate degree; and yet they called me, of all people. Who was I to have been blessed so? God knew what He was doing! By God's grace, this church called me with a 100 percent vote. Mercy!

We had two school principals in the church and a number of school teachers. As I continued to study and receive my education for ministry, Aubert Rose sent a packet of information to be filled out and mailed back to him in preparation for our first "Church Growth Revival." This was the greatest thing to happen to me in preparation for my future ministry. Because of my ignorance at that time, I tried to do it all. Not only did I fill out all the papers and turn them in to Aubert, the months of January through April were spent trying to put everything together.

During these four months, many of my senior saints informed me that they would probably unite with another church closer to their home or relatives. However, as a result of the wonderful week with Aubert, not one person left the church. To the contrary, everyone was so excited after that week! This was one of the greatest weeks of my ministry! That which I learned from Aubert Rose set the course for the direction God would lead me in the years ahead. We began our revival on a Wednesday night. This first service started out as "Sunday School Night." Thursday's service was "Men and Ladies Night." "Family & Youth Night" was on Friday. Saturday morning began with a "Gritz Blitz," as we enjoyed a full breakfast followed by a time of visiting in our community. Then, on Sunday morning, we had high attendance Sunday with a "SSSS" (Supernatural Sunday School Sunday) goal. This may not seem exciting to you, but for a church that had never experienced something like this, it was a very exciting day!

In the following pages, you will find a very organized and well-planned procedure to follow that will enable you to have one of these crusades. The pastor should never do this by himself, but he should find dedicated leaders who will assist him in developing a great team. There may be a very small number available to help, but it will be very exciting from beginning to end. Select your nucleus (remnant) and step out on faith. Delegate, pray and believe that God will do a work in your midst. Your church will refocus, learn and be prepared for the future. My advice is to first clear your calendar at least three months in advance, commit to prayer and planning, make your assignments, and enjoy the ministry!

Your best days can be ahead for church revitalization! When Nehemiah told his people how God had spoken to him and that God's hand was upon him, they responded by saying, "Let us rise up and build." They then strengthened their hands for this good work!

On the following pages, you will find a process I have used over the years in promoting a church revitalization crusade. This material is also sent to churches that have requested such a crusade. I trust that this material will help and bless you and your church. Pray over this and if I can assist you, please contact me at dannyb@churchrc.com.

Chapter Review: Planning a Church Revitalization Crusade

Nehemiah 2:18

Begin as Nehemiah
    Clear your calendar
    Plan the crusade three months in advance
    Commit to prayer and preparation
    Develop a team whose members are dedicated
    Make your assignments; delegate

Rise and build!
    Stand on God's words
    Expect opposition
    Believe God
    Go forward!

Church Revitalization Crusade
Preparation Materials

By Danny Burnley, D.Min., Consultant
513 Neely Ferry Road
Simpsonville, South Carolina 29680

Office: 864-918-3386
Email: dannyb@churchrc.com
Website: www. churchrc.com

Your crusade date is _____

What is a Church Revitalization Crusade?

Answer: A Church Revitalization Crusade derived from many years of experience and from one of my mentors, evangelist Aubert Rose. After numerous revivals under his leadership and after seeing the hand of God in the pastorate, I developed such a desire to help churches move from a stagnant, perhaps dying or visionless situation, to an exciting, vibrant, evangelical body that grows again!

This Revitalization Crusade can be used of God to remove hindrances to growth, catch a fresh vision, set challenging goals, deepen the commitment level of its leaders and stimulate God's people to work!

The right consultant will:
— Base everything on God's Word
— Challenge your people to pray and work more
— Lead in "Blitz Visitation"
— Share the abundant life in Jesus Christ
— Evaluate your Sunday school
— Look over your space
— Make recommendations in writing and leave with your pastor

A Church Revitalization Crusade will change a church if the church is ready!

Suggested Special Nights

Here are ways to build the Crusade attendance and get people into the services who need to make commitments.

Wednesday — Sunday School Night!

Assign pews to Sunday school workers, deacons and other leaders to fill. Award workers who have the largest number present. Urge 100 percent attendance in each class!

Thursday — Men and Ladies Night!

Assign all pews by numbers to men and women to fill with everyone they can — family members, church members, friends, neighbors, coworkers, etc. Award the man and woman who have the largest number present!

Friday — Family and Youth Night!

Assign all pews by numbers to families and urge them to have their entire family present. Award the family with the largest number present!

Saturday — Gritz Blitz!

Crusade Preparation

Step 1. Clear the church calendar completely. Two to three months should
be taken to get ready.

Step 2. Involve leadership. The more people you involve, the greater the
impact. The Sunday school director and leaders must take the
lead here. Go over this material with all church leaders. Commit
all Sunday school and other church leaders to attend all church
revitalization sessions. Urge everyone to attend and be involved!

Step 3. Pray. This is the key! No revival ever came about without prayer
and fasting! Claim Jeremiah 33:3!
- Lead the congregation to pray
- Lead all Sunday school teachers to pray
- Lead families to pray in their homes
- Lead in forming prayer partners
- Encourage personal, private (closet) praying
- Lead twelve-hour period of prayer and fasting before revival
from 6:00 a.m. until 6:00 p.m. (fasting from food only, not water)

Step 4. Tell the people. Start talking and writing about the crusade as soon
as it is scheduled, and intensify as the crusade approaches. Do
your best to get everyone to attend. Make copies of these plans
and share with all the Sunday school leaders and church members,
both active and inactive members.

Step 5. Music. Have musicians begin playing good gospel music at least
ten to fifteen minutes before the service. Prepare good, evangelistic
special music, solos, duets, ensembles, etc., and be prepared for
each service. Consider opening and closing with "Nothing is

Impossible!" (Luke 1:37). Keep announcements to a minimum during worship or wait until the end in order to keep a smooth flow of worship.

Step 6. Update your prospect file. Prospects are to be located, processed and assigned to all Sunday school units to insure growth. Between now and the revival services, names of prospects, addresses and phone numbers are a must. Begin now!

Conducting the Crusade

Step 1. Wednesday: Your guest consultant or preacher will arrive and get settled into the motel.

Step 2. Wednesday-Friday: Crusade services begin at 7:00 p.m., if possible, with pre-music before services. The guest consultant will be available to assist the pastor as he sees fit.

Step 3. Saturday morning "Gritz Blitz" schedule:
    8:45 a.m. — Full breakfast (please!)
    9:20 a.m. — Pastor explains packets and introduces consultant
    9:30 a.m. — Instructions
    10:00 a.m. — Visiting!
    11:30 a.m. — Return, fellowship, refreshments, reports, comments
    12:00 p.m. — Closing comments from pastor

Note: Visiting will not be done by Sunday school classes. Only one team will go to each house and invite all who live there to Supernatural Sunday School Sunday (SSSS)

Packets that contain seven different households with addresses as near to each other as possible will be assigned to each team of no more than three members. There should be at least one person at each address who was absent from Sunday school the previous Sunday, or who is a church member but not enrolled in Sunday school. Prepare enough packets, with a few extra, for the number of teams you anticipate to go out. Provide SSSS flyers announcing the Church Revitalization Crusade along with Sunday school enrollment cards to leave in the homes. Be sure to include the church name, address, phone number, pastor's name, SSSS goals and an invitation on the flyer.

(All preparations should be complete and ready by Thursday night for the Saturday visitation!)

Accommodations and Finances for the Consultant

What is my reward then? Verily that, when I preach the gospel, I may make the gospel of Christ without charge, that I abuse not my power in the gospel. (1 Corinthians 9:18)

1. I will never promote finances on my part.
2. If your church chooses to do so, a love offering may be taken at the end of each service.
3. Travel expenses and a good motel should be provided.

Who Will Help the Pastor?

Assignments:

Deacons — Each deacon should have a prayer at each service and should encourage everyone to pray, attend and invite others to the Church Revitalization Crusade. Excitement is contagious!

Sunday school director — The Sunday school director should immediately begin challenging each Sunday school class to set attendance goals, gather names to be contacted, and organize for outreach.

Men's leader — The men's director should organize a telethon to call all men of the church and prospects. Involve all men; assign men to make calls!

Ladies' leader — The ladies' director should organize a telethon to call all ladies of the church and prospects. Involve all ladies; assign ladies to make calls!

Youth leader — The youth leader should plan activities and contact all youth to become involved by inviting friends and relatives for high attendance day and revival.

Children's leader — Plan for children! Contact all children. Involve their teachers. Invite their parents, grandparents and friends!

Prayer captain — A prayer captain should be a prayer warrior already and an organizer. Begin a prayer chain for men and ladies. Pray! Pray! Pray!

Breakfast chairman — Have someone organize the best cooks and prepare the best breakfast for Saturday morning visitation. Have all to sign up for breakfast!

Worship leader — Make the most of worship! Keep announcements and prayer requests to a minimum during worship services. Let us worship and prepare for the Word!

Ushers — Enlist those who will meet, greet and seat our guests! Be friendly! Give directions. Inform parents with small children about the location of the nursery as they enter.

Telethon leader — Enlist capable volunteers to help organize, plan and prepare a telephone list of members and prospects and make calls encouraging their attendance. Calls will be made on Saturday afternoon before high attendance day.

High Attendance Day — Sunday of CRC Week
"SSSS" (Supernatural Sunday School Sunday!)

— Lead your people to set record-breaking goals for high attendance day. (Each class should set an attendance goal.)
— Emphasize and publicize class goals — begin now!
— Mail letter a week before the crusade from the pastor to all Sunday school class members, including all prospects and unenrolled church members, urging their attendance in Sunday school to help reach your goal!
— On Saturday morning (Gritz Blitz) visit all Sunday school absentees and unenrolled church members. Remember to prepare assignments with seven family units per assignment and group geographically.
— Prepare appropriate materials for Saturday "Blitz" to leave in all homes.
— Enroll everyone possible as visitation teams visit on Saturday.
— Provide a full breakfast before visitation on Saturday (8:45 a.m.) and light refreshments for report time in fellowship room after visitation (11:30 a.m.).
— Conduct telethon on Saturday afternoon to urge attendance. Pastor, call Sunday school director; director, call department directors; department directors, call teachers; teachers, call all class members!
— Enroll every visitor on SSSS who will agree to be enrolled; 50 percent will enroll if encouraged to do so.
— Recognize and reward all classes and workers who reach goals and others who work hard at this goal-setting week.
— Follow up by contacting the visitors who attended as well as new Sunday school members until they are attending regularly.
— Saturate with prayer and expect miracles!

Saturday Visitation Instructions: Be Polite!

— Remember, we are about our Father's business. (Jesus came to seek and to save that which was lost.)
— Team captains needed.
— Team captains will receive an envelope. DO NOT OPEN until teams are organized.
— Teams should have no more that two-to-three persons.
— Before departing, have envelope with visitor's cards, GPS or a map, and two flyers per visit.
— Upon arrival at the home, knock loudly. One should keep records.
— DO NOT GO INSIDE. We should all be back home by 12:00 noon.
— Give each family a flyer and tell them about high attendance day and the crusade.
— Give them an invitation to "come."
— Get a commitment. Let them know that we will be reporting all who will help us reach our goal on high attendance day.
— ALWAYS LEAVE A FLYER. DON'T FORGET!
— Records:
    Number of houses visited: _____
    Number of commitments: _____
    Possibilities: _____
    Number not at home: _____

Gritz Blitz

Welcome and Prayer

Thanks/Breakfast Committee

Table/Flyers — Envelopes/Maps

Team Captains Enlisted

    (___ # actually needed. If too many captains, divide envelopes by two)

Teams of Three

Instructions (after receiving envelopes, etc.)

Envelopes, number of flyers/instructions sheet

1. Pray first in the car.
2. Find the house.
3. Do not go inside.
4. One does the speaking. Be friendly!
5. Another keeps the records:

    How many houses visited _____

    How many at home _____

    How many committed to come _____
6. Give a flyer to each family.
7. Tell them about high attendance day goal in Sunday school at _____ a.m.
8. Tell them that we need their help in reaching this goal. Be excited! Just read your crusade flyer! Ask: Can we count on you to help us reach our goal? Write down the number of commitments.
9. Leave a flyer in the door if no one is home.
10. Return to the church with a report; turn in on table.
11. Invite others along the way.
12. Make phone calls to those who were not home.
13. Teachers: Contact absentees and prospects Saturday afternoon.

Telethon Script for Telethon Team
(Teams make calls before Crusade Week)

"Hello, this is _____ , and I am calling for _____
Baptist Church in _____ . The reason I am calling is because
we are beginning our Revitalization Crusade this Wednesday evening. We
are contacting all of our members and those who have visited with us to
encourage everyone to be in Sunday School at _____ a.m. and help us with
our High Attendance Day. Our goal is to have _____ in Sunday School. I
am excited about our crusade, and I want you and your family to be with
us! Can we count on you to be with us this Lord's Day?"

If the one who is called says no or is negative in any way, thank them
for their time and ask if they have any special prayer requests.

If they say yes, praise the Lord and ask the one to be present at _____
a.m. on Sunday and encourage them to bring someone with them.

*(Please list their names under the response listed below. Turn in to the
pastor.)*

YES   NO   MAYBE

Letter to Prospects
(Use church letterhead)

Dear Friend in Christ,

I would like to give you a *special invitation* to be in our services during our Church Revitalization Crusade beginning on _____ (date) through _____ (date).

We will have a High Attendance Day on Sunday, and I would like to encourage you to be with us in Sunday school at ____ a.m. Someone will meet you when you arrive and assist you in finding a class.

_____ (name of guest consultant) will be preaching nightly, Wednesday through Friday, at _____ p.m. and on Sunday at _____ a.m. and _____ p.m.

I do hope that you will make plans to worship with us. Bring your friends and your family as we trust God together for a great crusade!

Bring your Bible and join us we study God's Word and worship together. May God richly bless you!

Yours in Christ,

Sample Letter to Church Members
(On church letterhead)

To: All members/friends of _____ Church

From: Rev. _____, Pastor

Re: Church Revitalization Crusade

My Dear Friends,

I want to call upon every member and friend of _____ Church to join me in prayer and planning as we prepare for our Revitalization Crusade on _____ (date) and for our High Attendance Day in Sunday school on _____. Our goal for that Sunday in Sunday School is _____.

Begin now inviting others and by planning to be present for all services. The Bible says: "If my people who are called by My name shall humble themselves and pray, and seek My face, and turn from their wicked ways; then will hear from heaven, and will forgive their sin and will heal their land" (2 Chronicles 7:14).

Yours in Christ,

(Note: Mail a Crusade Flyer with this letter)

**Sample Letter to All Churches in Your Association
(On church letterhead)**

To: All Churches, _____ Association

From: Rev. _____, Pastor

My Dear Friends,

Will you please be so kind as to place this Church Revitalization Crusade flyer on your bulletin board and ask your members to pray for our church during these special services?

Thank you so much for your support in prayer. Come join us!

Yours in Christ,

(Note: Include a flyer with this letter)

Sample of "5 MOST WANTED!" List

5 MOST WANTED!

1. _____

2. _____

3. _____

4. _____

5. _____

CRC High Attendance Day
Goal: _____

About the Author: Danny Burnley

But God forbid that I should glory, save in the cross of our Lord Jesus Christ, by whom the world is crucified unto me, and I unto the world. (Galatians 6:14)

Served as youth Sunday school director, Sunday school teacher, Royal Ambassador director and youth director at age eighteen where I was saved and baptized at my home church

Licensed to preach in 1975 at Second Baptist Church, Thomson, Georgia; served as teacher, choir member, men's ministry director, chairman of the deacons

Ordained as pastor, Unity Baptist Church*, Vanna, Georgia, 1979-1983; served bi-vocationally while attending Emmanuel College, Franklin Springs, Georgia

Pastor, Union Baptist Church, Iva, South Carolina, 1983-1988

Pastor, Temple Baptist Church*, Simpsonville, South Carolina, 1988-2001

Pastor, Sierra Baptist Church*, Anderson, South Carolina, a new church start (upon the request of Delano McMinn, director of missions), 2001-2003

Pastor, West Gantt First Baptist Church*, Greenville, South Carolina, 2003-2011

Pastor, Laurel Baptist Church*, Greenville, South Carolina, 2011-2016

Church Revitalization Consulting, Inc. Upon my retirement as pastor on July 1, 2016, I began this new ministry with a desire to help churches experiencing decline

Churches that experienced restructuring and revitalization

Associational Involvement in South Carolina

President, Greater Iva Ministerial Association, Iva

President, Pastors' Conference, Saluda Baptist Association, Anderson

President, Pastors' Conference, and Moderator, Greenville Baptist Association, Greenville

Convention Involvement

Committee on Committees, South Carolina Baptist Convention (1992)

Registration secretary (1998), second vice president (2001), first vice president (2004) of South Carolina Baptist Convention

President of South Carolina Baptist Pastors' Conference (2007). Nearly $10,000 was raised at the Pastors' Conference for the Gideon Ministry.

Order of Business Committee (2002-2005), Executive Board (1998-2002), Nominating Committee and Chairman (1998-2001) for South Carolina Baptist Convention

Ministers Advisory Council, North Greenville College (2002-2005)

Ministers Advisory Council, Charleston Southern University (1996-2000)

Trustee, Anderson University (2006-2011)

Trustee, The Southern Baptist Theological Seminary, Louisville, Kentucky (1988-2004)

Board of Directors, Trinity Theological Seminary, Newburgh, Indiana. Received honorary doctorate for work in revitalizing churches.

Missions

Haiti — Served with missionary team from Elberton, Georgia, assisting Virgil Suttles, foreign missionary to Haiti.

Romania — Led six missionary trips to Romania while pastoring Temple Baptist Church, Simpsonville, South Carolina, completing two major building projects in Nassaud and in Tirgoviste.

CPSIA information can be obtained
at www.ICGtesting.com
Printed in the USA
LVOW01s1624170916
504806LV00004B/5/P

9 781940 645353